THE
SYDNEY HARBOUR
BRIDGE *A Life*

Born in Melbourne, Peter Spearritt first saw the Harbour Bridge when his parents took him to Sydney on a holiday in the early 1950s. Much of his collection of bridge souvenirs and photographs is now in the Museum of Sydney. A Professor of History at the University of Queensland, his books include *Sydney's Century*, which won the NSW Premier's prize for Australian history in 2000, and as co-author *Holiday Business: tourism in Australia since 1870* (2000) and *Electrifying Sydney* (2005). He has been a co-curator on a number of exhibitions including 'Australians and the Monarchy' and 'Triumph in the Tropics: selling Queensland'.

THE
SYDNEY HARBOUR
BRIDGE *A Life*

PETER SPEARRITT

NEWSOUTH

Contents

Front cover Poster, 'Still building Australia', 1930 by Percy Trompf, for the Australian National Travel Association, Public Record Office of Victoria

Back cover The southern arch in May 1930, showing the two sets of cables holding back the top chords. State Records New South Wales NRS12685

Endpapers Grahame Book Company, on the corner of Martin Place and Elizabeth Street commissioned Sydney printers, Edwards and Shaw to design and print this map of Sydney and its inhabitants in the early 1950s. At that time the heart of the city went from Circular Quay to Town Hall. Trams are still running at Circular Quay, because the city underground loop was yet to be completed. Banks and state government departments loom large in the landscape. Because of World War II the city hasn't changed much since the opening of the Bridge and the AWA Tower. The harbour is both a working port and a site of recreation, from Kings Cross to Luna Park, the Zoo and Manly. Spearritt collection

Page 2 Michael Leunig's take on Sydney in 1979, where the Bridge is accompanied by Sydney's two moons. Original drawing, not published at the time, Spearritt collection

Page 3 Handmade Australian Christmas shoe horn in beaten tin, 'for Milly from Dave'. (1940). Spearritt collection

Page 4 The majesty of Bridge steelwork. John Storey, 2006

Page 5 Neil Curtis was among a group of Melbourne graphic artists who enjoyed poking fun at Australian icons, as here in his 'The Revenge of the Calamari', postcard Cozzolino Hughes for Lamella Distribution, 1981

Page 6 Luna Park before opening time, with the Bridge as a spectacular backdrop. John Storey, 2006

Page 7 Brass bottle opener c 1982. Spearritt collection

Below Schools day on the Bridge proved a rainy affair, but that didn't deter this group of schoolgirls. State Records NSW NRS12685, 16 March 1932

Page 9 Poster artist Rhys Williams captures the grandeur of a P&O liner berthed at Circular Quay, c 1934

A NewSouth book

Published by
NewSouth Publishing
University of New South Wales Press Ltd
University of New South Wales
Sydney NSW 2052
AUSTRALIA
newsouthpublishing.com

© Peter Spearritt 2007
First edition published by George Allen and Unwin Pty Ltd, 1982.
New 75th anniversary edition 2007.
This revised edition 2011.

National Library of Australia
Cataloguing-in-Publication entry

Spearritt, Peter, 1949– .
 The Sydney Harbour Bridge: a life.

 Bibliography.
 Includes index.
 ISBN 9781742233086.
 1. Bridges, Arched - New South Wales - Sydney.
 2. Sydney Harbour Bridge (Sydney, N.S.W.).
 I. Title.
 624.22099441

Design Di Quick
Printer Everbest, China

to my parents, Jean and Don

Preface

In the mid-1920s Sydney became the first Australian city to boast a population of more than one million. A settler society, grown rich on gold, minerals and agricultural exports, could afford to import industrial technology, from locomotives to printing equipment. With the establishment of the BHP steelworks in Newcastle in 1915, Australia began to develop an industrial base that went beyond breweries and bakeries. Nonetheless, almost 80 per cent of the steel for the Sydney Harbour Bridge came from England.

Sydney's economy revolved around banking and insurance, wholesale and retail, small scale manufacture (from toasters to radios), food

∧ In the 1930s cartoonists satirised the bridge as Lang's Coathanger. For the 50th anniversary in 1982 a souvenir manufacturer produced this plastic coathanger. Spearritt collection

The PORT *of* SYDNEY

16   THE BRIDGE OF SIZE

THE BRIDGE CONCERT

"Or What You Will"

OVERTURE
"TO THE MINISTER" . . . . BARK
The Legislative Assembly Orchestra

SONG
"GOODBYE FOREVER" . . . . THEODORE
Rt. Hon. J. A. Lyons
Assisted by The Ten Little Australians

RECITATION
"NOT UNDERSTOOD" . . . . UMBUG
Tom Enley

THE AMAZING INTERLUDE—
"BALANCING THE BUDGET"
Featuring Sir Robar Gibbitsum
and
Long Tax Stan

THE BRIDGE OF SIZE   17

PART SONG
"THE MORE WE ARE TOGETHER" . . . BILLY YOUS
by
U.A.P., U.C.P., A.F.A.

Intermission—Time For a Quick'un

SONG AND DANCE
"THE BUSMAN'S HOLIDAY" . . . . . . F. H. STEWIT
The Transport Board

LIGHTNING SKETCHES . . . . MR. MARES

SONG
"SAID I TO MYSELF, SAID I" . . . . BRADFIELD
Maestro Freeman

COMIC SONG
"SHOW ME THE WAY TO GO HOME" . . . . . LANG
Sir Otto Niemeyer

MONOLOGUE
"THE TENTS OF ARABY" . . . . FOLD UP
Sam Walder

"THE RED FLAG"
Blight Street Choral Society
led by Mr. Archdale Parkhill

PROGRAMMES: PIANO:
SOVIET PRESS   HARRY MEATHERINGHAM

< The Port of Sydney regarded Port Jackson as its territory, Sydney c 1950. Spearritt collection

∧ The University of Sydney Labor Club sends up the key players at a tense and dramatic time in New South Wales politics. Bradfield is pitted against the Dorman

Long engineer, Freeman, while Premier Jack Lang is battling it out with Sir Otto Niemeyer of the Bank of England over Lang's refusal to repay British bondholders during the Great

Depression. There is no sign of de Groot as the students didn't have foreknowledge of that event. *The Bridge of Size*, Sydney, 1932. Spearritt collection

production, shipping, education and health. The city exported the agricultural produce of the State while most motor vehicles and manufacturing equipment were imported. The New South Wales government collected income tax, ran the railways, the tramways and the roads, and provided most of the schools and hospitals. The Commonwealth government, just 31 years old, had so little money

that when it built a provisional Parliament House in Canberra in 1927 it even used some fibro.

Australia's great 19th century structures were built on gold. The grandest – the Victorian Parliament House, the Exhibition buildings and the Hotel Windsor – were all in Melbourne. Sydney boasted a striking Town Hall but its Parliament stood in a street of left over and seemingly decrepit

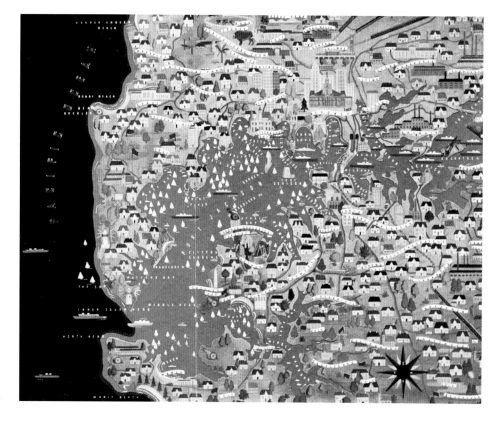

> Some sense of the significance of the Bridge to Sydney's geography can be gained from the Smith and Julius studios Bird's Eye View, c.1939, showing the extent of housing and industry on both sides of the harbour

> 'Here is a painter perched precariously on the top chord, engaged in giving the Bridge its protective covering of paint. His nerves are like the job he is working on – pure steel.' *Labor Daily* 9 February 1932

˅ Postcard showing the Warringah expressway, shortly after opening in 1968. Spearritt collection

convict structures. By the 1920s Circular Quay looked rundown with its warehouses and shipping companies, the convict built commissariat store and the Fort Bennelong Tram Terminus, now the site of the Opera House.

Rapid growth in a city that had outgrown horse-drawn vehicles and the tram and that seemed to have an unlimited supply of suburban building blocks put pressure on the State government to provide for an urban plan. Expanding and electrifying the railway system seemed the obvious answer. In stepped the diminutive Dr John Job Crew Bradfield, with a grand but realistic transport plan, the proposed bridge between Dawes Point and Milsons Point its symbolic and technological centrepiece.

More than half of Sydney's residents in the

1920s were tenants. Most men got a wage calibrated to support a wife and two children, while most women ceased paid work on marriage. There were pockets of great wealth, and also pockets of poverty, with unemployment at over 10 per cent for the whole decade. Very few workers got more than two weeks annual leave, so most leisure travel happened in and about Sydney. To escape the city, you boarded a train.

These were politically tense times. Governments lost office on average every two to three years. The leading politicians of the day loomed large, none larger than the commanding figure of Jack Lang, an Auburn real estate agent turned Labor politician, who understood the aspirations of working-class families to own their own home. Into this geographically divided and politically volatile landscape came the largest construction project that Australia had ever seen, a structure so bold in concept and design and so pivotal to transport in Sydney that it would capture the public imagination in a way that no other construction ever has.

∧ A Pylon Lookout hand-painted dish from Gluck pottery captures the sense of light and fun on Sydney Harbour in the mid 1960s. The recently opened overseas terminal (on left) is depicted in the abstract style popular at the time. This object was acquired on ebay on 19 December 2006, one day before the book went to the printers. Spearritt collection

Why a biography?

This biography traces the Bridge from concept, then building, to subsequent patterns of use. It is deliberately concise. Millions of words have been written about the Bridge since it opened. The State Archives of New South Wales holds the most important historical records, including plans and photographs, while the Mitchell Library and other repositories hold paintings, still photographs, moving footage, oral history and thousands of printed items. Major books about the Bridge and other key sources are listed in the bibliography.

When the first edition of this book appeared for the 50th anniversary in 1982, Sydney was undergoing a renaissance of self-confidence and artistic expression. Leading painters, graphic artists and photographers had rediscovered the majesty of the Bridge, celebrated by an earlier generation during construction.

> In December 1926 the British-produced *Meccano Magazine* celebrated the Bridge, using an artist's impression of what it might be like on completion, including landscaping at North Sydney

ᵛ The ferry terminal at McMahon's Point on 10 October 1930, with the deck in the first stages of being hung. State Records NSW NRS12685

VOL. XI. No.12   DECEMBER 1926

MECCANO MAGAZINE

THE LARGEST ARCH BRIDGE IN THE WORLD *see page 722*

6ᴰ

GARRISON CHURCH AND ARGYLE STREET, LOOKING TOWARDS THE HARBOUR BRIDGE

∧ The bridge from Argyle Place before the redevelopment of The Rocks. Postcard c 1961. Spearritt collection

walk from north to south, and weren't even allowed to walk back over the pedestrian walkway, which remained closed to the public on the day. This politically motivated attempt to limit the numbers walking received almost no press comment in either the *Sydney Morning Herald* or the local ABC radio station because both were locked in as 'sponsors' of the event. Such was the power of the bridge's symbolism that a government going to the polls could not risk any images of broken-down or overcrowded trains on its most visible and recognisable public structure.

The Bridge still joins the two halves of the city, just as it did in 1932. Motorists, train and bus commuters, pedestrians and cyclists use the Bridge day and night. The addition of a tunnel has increased road capacity, but the tunnel is out of sight, in a trench on the harbour floor.

More and more of our great structures are privately owned, from tollways to skyscrapers. The Bridge remains firmly in public hands. While the wealthy gazump each other in the harbour real estate market to view it, anyone can walk or cycle across without payment. Even highly paid city executives haven't been able to completely monopolise the Bridge view from their offices and boardrooms. Public parks on both sides of the harbour provide marvellous viewing points, as does Circular Quay and the Botanic Gardens. A little further afield the Bridge can be viewed from Bradley's Head. To the west, Balls Head, Longueville and Balmain offer different perspectives. All these sites are crowded for the New Year's Eve bridge foreworks, broadcast around the world. That arch of steel on the horizon can still be seen as far away as Bankstown and North Head.

To the surprise of the State government, who gave permission for the Bridge to be closed to traffic – making the roadway available to the public for the first time since the opening in 1932 – up to 500 000 people walked across it. The Department of Main Roads had predicted 50 000.

In May 2000, the bridge again fulfilled a symbolic role when the organisers of the People's Walk for Reconciliation persuaded the state government to close it to traffic, so the walk could symbolise a bridge between Indigenous Australians and the white majority. The spontaneity and hope that marked that occasion was completely lost at the 75th anniversary in March 2007, when the troubled Labor government led by Maurice Iemma, beset by public transport woes, fearful of terrorist attack and facing an election just six days later, implemented an absurd level of control. People had to register to walk, were only allowed to

Acknowledgments

Friends and colleagues have tolerated my fascination with the Bridge over the last 35 years. Some have even encouraged it with additions to my Bridge collection, much of which was donated to the Museum of Sydney in 2003. Successive occupants of 2/14 Hayes Street Neutral Bay became part-time curators. Colleagues at Macquarie, the Australian National University, Monash and the University of Queensland may now see the bridge as part of the resurgence of a national narrative.

As a university student I was privileged to interview Jack Lang, New South Wales premier at the time of the opening, to talk to bridge workers, engineers and maintenance workers, and to meet some of the Bridge's great artistic interpreters, from Wep (Bill Pidgeon) and Emerson Curtis to Brett Whiteley, Peter Kingston and Martin Sharp.

I owe a special debt to my parents, who moved house from Melbourne to Sydney in 1960. John Iremonger (1944–2002) nurtured the first edition of this book, as did Adrian Young. Bob Mack, Glenn Cooke, Anne Gilmore, Denise Dufferin, Stephen Foster, John Young and Benedict Spearritt have assisted in subsequent editions. John Storey, who photographed the Bridge for me in 1981, did so again in 2006. At UNSW Press Phillipa McGuinness and Di Quick oversaw this third edition.

Staff at the Roads and Traffic Authority, the current custodian of the Bridge, have been unfailingly helpful. I am grateful to a number of individuals and organisations who have allowed me to reproduce material in their collections and granted copyright permission where necessary. They are acknowledged in the captions on p. 171.

< Looking towards North Sydney from the top of the western side of the Bridge. Luna Park still has its Big Dipper ride. Almost all the tall buildings are office blocks, but since this photgraph was taken by John Storey in 1981 highrise apartment blocks have been added to the landscape

ᵥ Postcard manufacturers chose a number of vantage points from which to depict the bridge. Postcard c 1938 Spearritt collection

A harbour crossing

In 1791 when Dr Erasmus Darwin penned his poem 'Visit of Hope to Sydney-Cove, near Botany-Bay', the new European settlement was heavily forested, save for a handful of straggling convict settlements. Thousands of Aborigines were living in the Sydney region, sustained by abundant animal life and shellfish.

Conrad Martens,
Sydney from the North
Shore, 1842, lithograph,
watercolour on paper,
Art Museum, University
of Queensland. When
Martens composed this
scene Circular Quay and
the Rocks were already
well developed, but the
North Shore remained
sparsely settled, still
home to some Aborigines

By 1924, when work began on the 'proud arch' that was to become known as the Sydney Harbour Bridge, Sydney was the busiest port in Australia. Erasmus Darwin's vision of 'embellish'd villas' and 'tall spires' was, if anything, an understatement. Sydney's population had grown from a few thousand Europeans and many more Aborigines – who were sometimes brutally dispersed to the hinterland – to over a million, earning it the title of 'second white city of Empire'. With these facts of progress and achievement being paraded in the press throughout the interwar years, the Sydney Harbour Bridge was hailed as a 'masterpiece' of Australian workmanship and British engineering, proof of just how far Australia had come since its first convict settlement.

The idea of a bridge linking Sydney Cove with the North Shore had been the gleam in many a would-be prophet's eye. In 1815 the emancipated convict and government architect, Francis Greenway, proposed a bridge from Dawes Point to the North Shore, but produced no plans. In 1857 an engineer trained in George Stephenson's locomotive workshops in England produced the first known drawing of a bridge connection, while in 1878 WC Bennett, Commissioner for Roads and Bridges, advocated the erection of a pontoon from Dawes Point to Milsons Point to carry vehicles, passengers and possibly a railway train. The following year JS Parrott prepared a sketch design of a truss bridge

Sydney from the North Shore – 184

< David Moore's aerial photograph captures Port Jackson, Sydney Harbour and the Parramatta River. The basic structure of the waterway is not much altered from 1788, but this 1992 photograph makes the pivotal role of the Harbour Bridge abundantly clear. David Moore 'Sydney Harbour from 20 000 feet'

> The front cover of this 1913 booklet showed 'natives opposing the landing of Captain Cook'. Prior Aboriginal occupation of Australia was much more likely to be acknowledged pictorially than in text at this time. Fryer Library, University of Queensland

of seven spans, the longest span being 150 metres.

In the 1880s the linking of Sydney and North Sydney became a major political issue. At the beginning of the decade the New South Wales government opened negotiations with JE Garbett, who represented a company that proposed to construct a high-level bridge at a cost of £850 000. In October 1881 the Colonial Premier, Sir Henry Parkes, signed a Cabinet minute agreeing to Garbett's proposal and in March 1882 Garbett deposited £5000 as security. Parkes' coalition lost the election, so Garbett's bridge did not proceed. From this time proposals were put forward with increasing regularity, and political pressure grew so intense that between 1890 and 1909 a harbour crossing was the subject of two Royal Commissions and an advisory board report. A bridge was not seen as the only possible solution; many people favoured the idea of a tunnel instead.

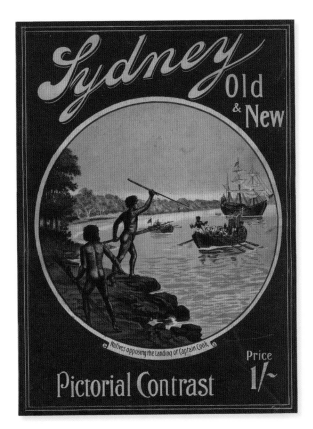

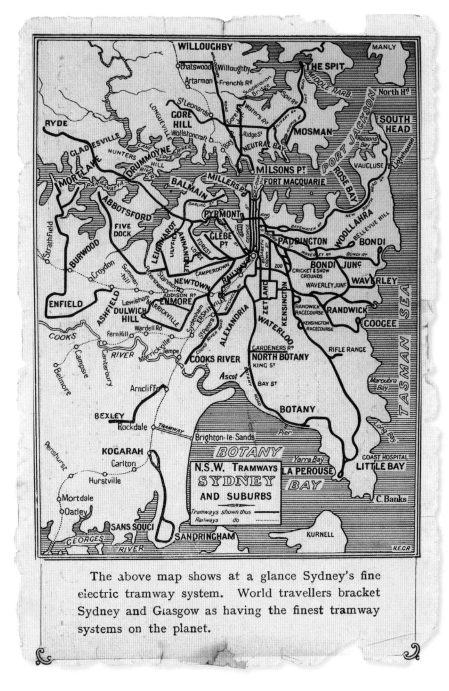

The above map shows at a glance Sydney's fine electric tramway system. World travellers bracket Sydney and Glasgow as having the finest tramway systems on the planet.

∧ By 1914 Sydney had an extensive rail and tramway system, radiating out from the city centre. Apart from passenger and vehicular ferries, residents and visitors could only cross the harbour at the Gladesville Road Bridge or on the railway bridge, further west. *Trips about Sydney*, Government Tourist Bureau, 1914

Tunnel or bridge?

A tunnel connection to North Sydney, proposed in 1885, providing for both rail and horse-drawn vehicles, floundered over how it would be financed. In January 1888 a deputation waited upon Parkes to urge the construction of a bridge to mark the Centenary of the colony of New South Wales. Three years earlier he had contested and won the seat of St Leonards with the election slogan

> *Now who will stand at my right hand*
> *And build the Bridge with me?*

Centennial Park, being a relatively cheap commemorative venture, got priority over a bridge, not least because the eastern suburbs were more populous and had more political power than the northern suburbs. After further agitation a Royal Commission was appointed in 1890 to inquire

whether the North Shoreline railway should be extended and how the link between the city and North Sydney might be made. The Commission received eight submissions for a bridge, fewer for a tunnel. While it concluded that action was not yet necessary, it recommended a high-level bridge, preferably a single span to avoid interference with shipping.

In the following years a number of schemes were suggested and four bills were presented to Parliament, including two for a tunnel link (promoted by the immigrant English architect, John Sulman, after whom the art prize is named) and two for a bridge. Although none of these schemes

<^ Proposed tunnel entrance and tunnel carriages, *Sydney Mail* 30 May 1896. Such tunnels, especially for trains, were being dug in many major cities at the turn of the century

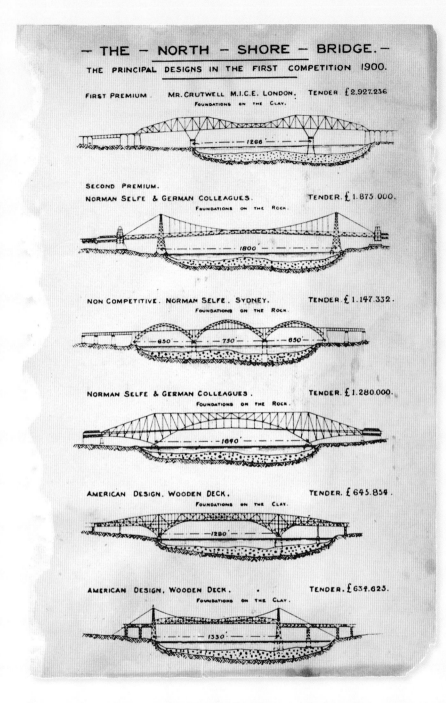

reached fruition, pressure from interested parties continued to mount. In 1898 a deputation including representatives from North Sydney, Willoughby, Lane Cove and Mosman councils demanded construction of a bridge, a cheeky demand, as three of the municipalities had only recently come into being, and between them represented fewer that 40 000 people. However they included in their number a high proportion of the professional classes who, having discovered the leafy delights of the North Shore, were moving there in droves. Subdivisions sprang up overnight and land prices rose steadily. After further deputations, including one calling itself 'The People's Bridge League',

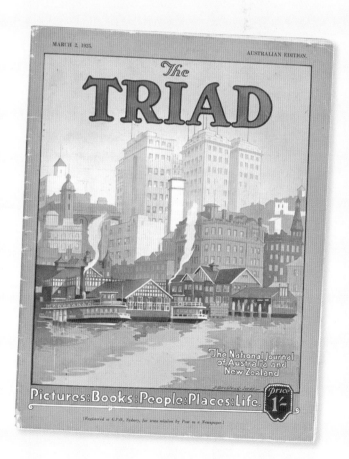

∧ The harbour crossing competition in 1900 drew an array of bridge designs and tender prices, reflecting trends in bridge construction in the United States and Britain

> The March 1925 *Triad* magazine depicts Circular Quay with its Edwardian wharves and warehouses and some fanciful new blocks in the style of the Astor Flats, which had been recently erected on Macquarie Street. Local residents and business people knew that a Bridge would change the face of Circular Quay forever

EW O'Sullivan, the Minister for Public Works, called for competitive designs and tenders. Twenty-four designs were received, including some which would stretch the imagination of any engineer, but none were considered satisfactory. The following year O'Sullivan appointed an advisory board, chaired by an engineer, which called for a new round of tenders. In November 1903 this board recommended the adoption of Stewart and Co's design for a cantilever bridge from Dawes Point to McMahons Point, having a span of 411 metres between piers. Prepared by a local engineer, Norman Selfe, in conjunction with two German firms, this design provided for a 10-metre roadway, two tram tracks, two rail tracks, and a 3-metre-wide footway. Unfortunately for the tenderers, who had gone to considerable effort and expense in the preparation of their scheme, New South Wales was in the midst of a minor recession and no further action was taken.

By the early 1900s the need to link Sydney with North Sydney had become a hardy perennial of Sydney politics. The promise of such a connection had helped Henry Parkes win and retain the seat of St Leonards (which covered most of the lower North Shore) in 1885. Many a municipal politician, egged on by local real estate interests, had a bridge or tunnel proposal as part of his platform. In 1908, under pressure from the Sydney and North Sydney Bridge League, yet another Royal Commission was convened on the subject. Royal Commissions had become a useful tool for governments who wished to be seen to be doing something.

The Commission was asked how to best link Sydney with North Sydney while avoiding obstruction to harbour navigation. Commission witnesses told of the rapid growth of population of the northern side of the harbour, increasing at 10 per cent per annum compared with only 3 per cent for the city and suburbs overall. The Bureau of Statistics predicted that the area would continue to grow at 6 per cent per annum for the next 20 years. Though occupied dwellings numbered only 13 000, the capital value of the North Shore municipalities and shires was estimated at over £10 000 000. Traffic on its new railway, from Milsons Point to St Leonards and on to Hornsby, opened in 1893, practically doubling in six years. The veneer of economic rationality (especially in the absence of any proper costing) and the air or progress that such statistics conveyed were to prove vital when Parliament finally passed the *Sydney Harbour Bridge Act* in 1922.

The ferry and shipping interest

The Commission received a number of complaints from ferry passengers about overcrowding and the dangers of embarking and disembarking. At any one hour in peak periods 75 ferries were docking or in the water. The five major ferry services which then linked the city with the North Shore accounted for 13 million passengers per year. Understandably, the ferry companies were bitterly opposed to the proposed link, because it would remove much of their patronage. Sydney Ferries Limited, which had the bulk of the trade, also ran two vehicular steam ferries, between Dawes Point and Blues Point and between Bennelong Point and Milsons Point. In the early 1900s the great majority of the vehicles were horse-drawn, as motor cars had only recently arrived in Sydney from overseas.

The port of Sydney, as contemporary photographs show, was a hive of activity. Steam-powered ferry boats plied through the harbour waters with apparent ease, though they did become overcrowded at the beginning and end of each working day. To the ferry passengers of the early 1900s the notion of a giant bridge linking the shores of the harbour seemed quite fanciful. Regular ferry services had begun in the 1850s and by the end of the century they were a familiar part of Sydney's landscape.

A considerable amount of freight had to cross the harbour, especially foodstuffs and building materials to keep pace with the fast-growing suburbs. Many of the horse-drawn vehicles – especially if they were high or wide or in other ways cumbersome – could not use the vehicular ferries and had to divert by way of the Gladesville Bridge, which had opened in 1881. With only two lanes it soon became a bottleneck. (The even more distant Ryde Bridge was not opened till the mid-1930s.) A horse-drawn freight trip from the city centre via Gladesville to North Sydney could take many hours.

<v These bridge designs by Norman Selfe, one a cross-section and the other a longitudinal view, were approved by the Advisory Board in 1903, but Selfe's proposal suffered the same fate as all earlier designs, and did not proceed beyond the design phase. Mitchell Library, Small Picture File

< Before the Bridge, vehicular ferries carried horse-drawn passenger and freight vehicles. By the 1920s cars and trucks were becoming more common. Kirribilli terminal, 1931. Photograph by EO Hoppe

As in 1900, this new Royal Commission received some very far-fetched schemes for connecting the city with North Sydney. George Pile presented a scheme which did not belie his surname, for a low-level wing bridge for tram and vehicular traffic (but not trains), from Balls Head via Goat Island and Balmain to Pyrmont. Like many other schemes it was rejected because it would impede navigation. John Sulman, who by this time was one of the city's best known architects and

Macquarie to Moore Street, one for trams and one for vehicular traffic, both to follow the same route from Arthur Street North Sydney via Milsons Point to Dawes Point. It concluded that subways had three advantages over a bridge: the harbour would not be obstructed by piers, subways cost less and rail, tram and vehicular traffic would be separated from each other.

Into this morass of Royal Commission and advisory boards, with their contradictory recommendations, stepped JJC Bradfield. A young engineer who had risen rapidly through the ranks of the Public Works Department, Bradfield possessed – unusually for an engineer – that rare combination of technical ability, aesthetic good sense (at least as perceived by his peers) and political nous that is the mark of a successful public works bureaucrat. He had seen how Parliament and the bureaucracy worked and he knew the instrumental value of consensus. He developed a flair for public relations and political negotiation. Introducing an ill-fated Sydney Harbour Bridge Bill to the Legislative Council in April 1916, the housing reformer and town planning advocate JD Fitzgerald told his colleagues:

> The history of this bridge is the history of our politics for the last forty years. This bridge has been the sport of politicians for the whole of that period ... [it will] open up those splendid areas of undulating land which are so admirably suited for the purpose to which they have since been applied, namely, the building of homes for citizens, the housing of the happy and healthy people on that side of the Harbour ... Mr Bradfield has a mastery of the subject. He has travelled the world, he has made this his special study ... We can leave this to him; it will be his life's work ... our great engineer has devised a scheme in which he has worked out details to the last bolt in the bridge.

∧ In the late 1920s Sydney's ferries achieved their highest patronage levels ever, carrying over 45 000 000 passengers a year. Today they carry about 15 000 000, but are still central to Sydney's self-image. The ferry and tram terminus at McMahons Point on the northern side of the harbour. Erection Wages, 1932

'town planning' advocates, reiterated his earlier support for subways, arguing that the functions required of the bridge would make it too huge to be aesthetically pleasing, and given the State's commitment to other large public enterprises – including the Barren Jack Dam and the Broken Hill rail line – too expensive. The Commission ended up recommending three subways: one for rail from Lavender Bay via Kirribilli Point and Fort

The Bradfield plan for Sydney

*The construction of the city underground railway and — much
more spectacularly - of the Sydney Harbour Bridge were the
great events of interwar Sydney. They were structures with political,
social, moral and economic overtones which went well beyond their
immediate physical impact on the city. The name most closely associated
with both of these developments was that of John Job Crew Bradfield.*

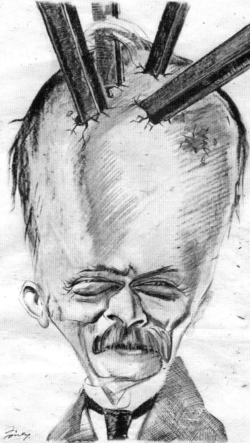

Bradfield was born on 26 December 1867 at Sandgate, Queensland, fourth son of John Edward Bradfield, labourer and Crimean War veteran, and his wife Maria, née Crew. They arrived in Brisbane from England (with their three eldest children) in 1857, moving to Ipswich in 1859 where Bradfield senior set up a brick making business in the thriving town. Educated at the North Ipswich State School and the Ipswich Grammar School on a scholarship, Bradfield passed the Sydney senior public examination in 1885, gaining the medal for chemistry. Dux of his school, he won a Queensland government scholarship to the University of Sydney, there being no university in Queensland at that time. From St Andrew's College he continued his brilliant academic career, graduating with a Bachelor of Engineering and the University Gold Medal in 1889.

Back in Brisbane Bradfield worked as a draughtsman under the Chief Engineer of Railways. In the depression of 1891 he was retrenched and joined the New South Wales Department of Public Works as a temporary draughtsman, becoming permanent in 1895. An associate from 1893 of the Institution of Civil Engineers, London, he went on to acquire a Master of Engineering with first class honours and the University Medal from the University of Sydney in 1896. He had been a founder of the Sydney University Engineering Society in 1895 and was president in 1902–03 and 1919–20. In his 1903 presidential address he drew attention to the competition initiated in 1900 for the design of a bridge across Sydney Harbour.

The new transport developments were a central concern of the ambitious Royal Commission of 1909 on the improvement of Sydney and its suburbs. In that year Bradfield put forward his first scheme for the city railway to the Public Works Department. This initiative, and his excellent academic qualifications, were undoubtedly factors in the decision of the Labor Public Works Minister to appoint him, in July 1912, as the engineer in charge of the newly created Sydney Harbour Bridge

as many plates, it included chapters on the city railway, the 'Sydney Harbour Bridge Problem', suburban electrification, the tramways, and the 'The Population, Commerce and Passenger Traffic of Sydney'.

Bradfield, aware that a Railway Bill was soon to come before Parliament, went to considerable effort in his 1915 report to show the practicality of his scheme. He was at his most convincing in this report (as in all his later publications) when

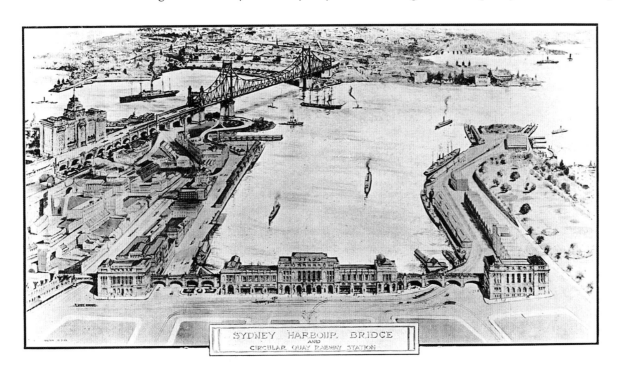

< A cantilever harbour bridge and classical Circular Quay station as envisaged by Bradfield in 1923. The decision to call tenders for an arch as well as a cantilever bridge came shortly after. *Ceremony of Turning the First Sod, Northern Side,* 1923

< Though short in stature, Bradfield, with his massive cranium, was instantly recognisable. George Finey, Australia's greatest caricaturist, always took a physical feature of his subject and enlarged it, hence Bradfield's cranium sprouting steel girders. *Art in Australia,* June 1931

and City Transit Branch. From this time Bradfield's fame and influence grew. In 1914 he was sent to Great Britain, Europe and North America by the Labor government to investigate new approaches to metropolitan railway construction and long span bridge construction and in February the following year he submitted his *Report on the Proposed Electric Railways for the City of Sydney.* Comprising 76 pages of facts, figures and recommendations, and

he managed to combine both the factual and the symbolic aspects of his plan. His talent for public relations played a part in the passage of the Labor-sponsored City and Suburban Electric Railways Bill of 1915, when Bradfield's scheme came under close scrutiny. The key debates took place in the Legislative Council, since the Labor majority in the Assembly assured the Bill a relatively easy passage there. The Bill passed the Legislative Council because of the consensus which developed between key Labor and non-Labor members. There were a number of reasons for this agreement: a desire to reduce traffic congestion by introducing a planned transit system, the revenue that the system was predicted to gain, and the universally acknowledged professional expertise of Bradfield.

The Sydney Harbour Bridge Bill encountered a different fate, primarily because it did not reach the Legislative Council until April 1916. The Great War was by this time the centre of attention, and imperial loyalty and concern for war finances defeated the Bridge proposal. Bradfield's plan received another setback in June 1917 when Cabinet decided to discontinue the city railway, in part because of the collapse of the financial agreement with the London-based Norton Griffiths and Company in March 1917, entered into originally because of the difficulty of obtaining loan funds. In 1915 restricted finances had already led the Railway Commissioners to postpone suburban electrification for five years.

In the years following the June 1917 decision to postpone the city railway, Bradfield mounted a publicity campaign in support of his plan. At the first Australian Town Planning Conference held in Adelaide in October 1917, he took the opportunity to present a paper on 'The Transit Problems of Greater Sydney'. Bradfield marshalled many arguments for proceeding with his scheme, and they were accompanied by an array of graphs and sketches of the Sydney of the future. The core of his scheme was suburban electrification, a city underground railway and a bridge to link the city proper with the northern suburbs. He set out to appeal to a coalition of interests. Chief amongst these was his claim to provide for the residential needs and aspirations of the population, including 'workers':

> with the scheme proposed there should be a more efficient service, a reduction in working expenses, cheaper fares and quicker transit, thus enabling workers to reside further afield and enjoy fresh air and sunlight.

He also appealed to both property owners and local government by arguing that they would benefit 'materially' from increased land values and increased council rates. Nor did he neglect the aesthetic aspects, claiming that 'the various structures will be in architectural harmony with their surroundings'.

Bradfield backed up his arguments with statistical tables, a classic tool of persuasion for the 'apolitical' expert. One projected the growth of

∨ The south portal of the proposed cantilever bridge. Electric trains are running on both sides of the structure, with an expected completion date of 1931. *Ceremony of Turning the First Sod, Northern Side,* 1923

CANTILEVER BRIDGE
SOUTH PORTAL

CHIEF ENGINEER
SYDNEY HARBOUR BRIDGE
PLAN N°
24

Sydney's population to the year 1950, claiming that it
should on a conservative basis reach 2 226 000, while
the other showed projected growth rates of various
types of mass transport. Such projections indicate
Bradfield's great confidence in the future progress of
the city and in his own ability for forward planning;
a confidence that others were soon to share. As
Bradfield planned it, the Bridge was to be primarily
a railway bridge for commuters between the city
centre, where most of the jobs were, and the North
Shore. The roadway was to be used for horse-drawn
and vehicular freight and recreational trips in cars
for the few who could afford them.

Bradfield sustained publicity for his scheme
through a variety of publications, always
tailored to the needs of audience, whether town
planners, engineers, the mass reading public
or the government. In mid-1921 he addressed
the New South Wales Institute of Architects on
the 'Sydney Harbour Bridge'. The address was
reprinted in the October issue of George Taylor's
Building ('the magazine of interest to the builder,
engineer and architect'). Beginning in December
1921 he published three articles in the popular
journal *Sea, Land, Air* on his transit schemes for

Sydney. They included a revised plan for his
suburban electrification scheme, similar to the one
reproduced here. This time a St Leonards–Eastwood
railway had been added to further open up the
'healthy' residential lands of the North Shore. The
final article of the *Sea, Land, Air* series appeared in
February 1922, seven months before Parliament
was due to debate the Sydney Harbour Bridge. It
was called 'World's Heaviest Steel Structure: How
It Will Appear When Completed'. The title should
realistically have read 'if built', but Bradfield was an
aggressive salesman; his mixture of self-confidence
and tenacity was soon to be rewarded.

On 17 February 1922, after a 4½-year lapse,
work finally began again on excavations for the city
underground railway. The Labor government had
come under considerable pressure both from the
Railway Commissioners and from eastern suburbs
municipalities to recommence the project. Until
that time, so Treasury papers suggest, there had
been great problems raising the necessary finance.
The Railway Commissioners were concerned that
if the city railway didn't proceed promptly their
passengers would be left on the Milsons Point side
of the Bridge.

The Sydney Harbour Bridge Act

The real test for Bradfield came in the 1922 debates on the Sydney Harbour Bridge Bill, the centrepiece of his plan for Sydney. A move to introduce the Sydney Harbour Bridge Bill had already been made by the Dooley Labor government in 1921, but that government lost office before the Bill had proceeded very far. The Labor government had, however, sent Bradfield overseas to inquire about tenders for a cantilever bridge. He met leading American bridge engineers in Chicago, and visited Quebec where a cantilever bridge had collapsed in 1907, and saw its replacement, the world's longest cantilever bridge, opened in 1918. The incoming government attempted to recall him by sending a cable to New York, but tipped off by his secretary, Kathleen Butler, Bradfield avoided receiving the cable, and left early for England. The new premier wanted him to see if there would be any interest in a toll-based payment scheme for tenderers (in effect an early version of the Sydney Harbour Tunnel financing) but Bradfield firmly discouraged that approach, on the grounds that potential tenderers would lose interest in the project.

By July, heavily influenced by a technical report on the arch design used in the Hell Gate Bridge in New York, completed in 1916, Bradfield became enthusiastic about the prospects of an arch, suggesting that it should also be included as an option in a new draft of the *Sydney Harbour Bridge Act*. On the ship home he became convinced, after extensive calculations, that an arch bridge would be cheaper and use less steel than the cantilever design.

In September 1922 the Bill was reintroduced by the Nationalist Secretary for Public Works, RT Ball:

Mr Bradfield is looked upon not only in Australia but in the engineering profession throughout the world, as one of the most competent men associated with bridge work, and I do not know of any man who would be better qualified to advise the government in regard to the bridge.

< RT Ball, the Minister for Public Works at the time of the passage of the Bridge bill, after whom Balls Head at North Sydney is named. George Finey, *Art in Australia*, June 1931

Dooley put the Labor view:

I am in favour of the construction of the bridge … I consider it is right that two such important and extensive portions of the city should be connected. When that connection is made, and trains are running over the bridge, some of the finest residential country within twenty minutes of the city will be opened.

Bradfield stood at the centre of the emerging consensus between Labor and the Nationalists, his engineering expertise unquestioned, at a time when engineers were held in high esteem as nation builders. The Nationalists living on the North Shore foresaw the increase in property values and greater accessibility to the city that the Bridge would bring. Ten years later the *Labor Daily* commented on the 'influence of home owners and land speculators in the charming and healthy northern suburbs' and pointed out that:

> another factor operating when the authorising bill was put through was the rising importance of members from the northern side of the Harbour in the inner workings of the Nationalist Party, and the necessity to placate them.

Many in the Labor Party hoped that the Bridge link would open up – for the first time in the history of Sydney's working class – the residential areas on the North Shore, because it would mean that they could get to the shops, warehouses and factories in and to the south and west of the city centre.

The main opposition to the Bridge came from the Progressive Party, precursors of the Country Party. Their deputy leader, David Henry Drummond, told Parliament:

> I say it is wrong to build the city railway and the North Shore bridge when we want railways

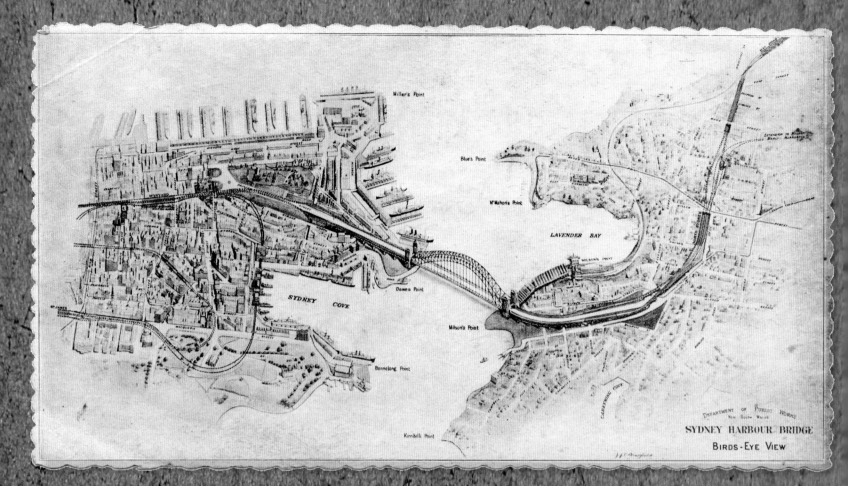

SYDNEY HARBOUR BRIDGE

BIRDS-EYE VIEW

^ Department of Public
Works map, signed by
Bradfield, gives a bird's
eye view of the Bridge and
the new railway stations
being built at North Sydney,
Milsons Point and for the
city underground loop. The
Dorman Long workshops
can be seen abutting the
existing Milsons Point
railway station, on Lavender
Bay. *Sydney Harbour Bridge
and city railway*, Phillips,
Willoughby, 1927

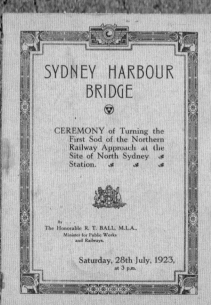

< The commemmorative
booklet for the ceremony
of the turning of the first
sod of the northern railway
approach had the cantilever
bridge logo on its back
cover. All the North Shore
municipalities were
represented, and models of
the Bridge were presented
to Ball and Bradfield.
A banquet starting at 4pm
ended with guests singing
'Advance Australia Fair'
having already toasted
The King, the NSW
Parliament, and Bradfield
as 'the designer of the
Bridge'. NSW Government
Printer, July 1923, Spearritt
collection

Hell Gate Bridge, New York City.

< The Hell Gate Bridge in New York, built for the Pennsylvania Railroad Company between 1912 and 1917, linking interstate trains to Manhattan Island. Its 1000 foot clear span made it the largest arch bridge in the world, attracting the interest of engineers because of its size and weight carrying capacity

outback … The North Shore bridge would undoubtably confer a great benefit. I recognise it as a necessary work, but it is not so vital to the progress and well being of New South Wales as the works which I have mentioned.

The Progressives did not question the Bridge or the Bradfield plan as such, but rather where the money was spent. Their criticism left unruffled the basic agreement that existed between Labor and the Nationalists, including rural members of both those parties. The Bridge Bill's leading advocate, RT Ball, with a mechanical engineering background, was the Nationalist member for the New South Wales border seat of Murray.

In the second reading debate of 10 October 1922 Ball continued to promote Bradfield and his expertise, which Bradfield himself had been busily doing, making, as the *Bulletin* observed, many appearances in the lobbies and party rooms of Parliament House. Ball told members of

the return of Mr Bradfield, who is present tonight

> The first seal for the Bridge reflects the assumption, current when the *Bridge Act* passed in 1922, that a cantilever structure would be erected. *Ceremony of turning the first sod, northern side*, 1923

He is designer of the bridge, and the man who has had all to do with the preparation of the plans and specifications … I am going to ask the House to amend the conditions so as to provide that it may be either a cantilever or an arch bridge. That will give us an opportunity of considering tenders which Mr Bradfield says are likely to be received owing to the fact that there has been a development this year in the manufacture of steel unknown to builders a few years ago, but which it has now been proved can be applied to bridge building. It will enable a great reduction in the weight of steel used.

35

The tenders: cantilever or arch?

Under the terms of the *Sydney Harbour Bridge Act* of 1922, tenders were invited for cantilever and arch bridges in accordance with 'official designs' as provided by the Chief Engineer, Mr Bradfield. Tenderers were invited to submit independent designs, but a few did produce plans for suspension bridges and Bradfield stated that he gave these tenders the same 'careful' consideration as for arch and cantilever designs. Twenty tenders were received from six companies.

The most expensive tender came from the Goninan Bridge Corporation in Newcastle-Upon-Tyne, England. For £10 112 000 they offered to a build a 'cantilever suspension' bridge. In his comments Bradfield pointed out that a bridge of this type had not yet been built and concluded that the Goninan tender was 'the highest of all the tenders received; neglecting price the bridge had nothing to commend it as regards design, appearance or fabrication in Australia'.

The English Electric Co of Australia Ltd produced three tenders, within the price range of £4 944 000 to £5 609 000. All three were for stiffened suspension bridges. The designs were prepared by a New York engineering firm and modelled on that of a bridge built in Manheim, Germany, in 1887. Bradfield regarded this as a 'novel' design, more rigid than any 'existing suspension bridge' but he thought that rigidity had been obtained by 'sacrificing beauty of outline in the stiffening truss'. Moreover, he argued, 'there is a tendency for the cables and suspenders of a suspension bridge to vanish from view on account of their slimness, when seen from a moderately distant view'. In this comment we see his understanding of what the 'public' expect in a bridge, particularly a bridge that is to join the two halves of their city. They expect a structure that not only stays up but looks as though it will stay up.

The McClintic Marshall Products Company hedged their bets even more than the English Electric Co, producing five tenders which ranged in

io   SYDNEY HARBOUR BRI

THE MIN

Left to R
Mr.

price from £5 655 00 to £6 499 00. Three tenders were for a cantilever bridge, one for an 'inverted arch' and one for a three-hinged arch. Bradfield complained that their cantilever designs were 'unhandsome', 'too utilitarian' and cost too much. Their inverted arch design was a three-hinged cable suspension rather like those considered for the Quebec Bridge in Canada and the Hell Gate Bridge in New York, but it was discarded in both cases. Bradfield thought that the company's last proposal, for a three-hinged braced arch, was marred by its appearance: 'the defined crescent shape of each half-arch does not produce a satisfactory optical explanation of the transference of the enormous stress from the crown of the arch to the abutments at the springings'.

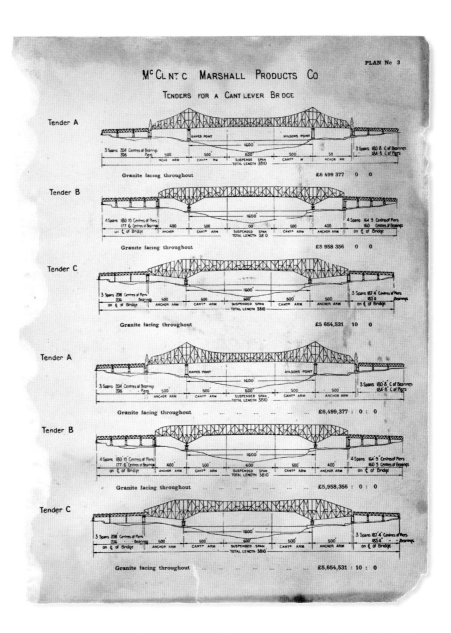

SOUVENIR. II

TILEVER BRIDGE FROM DAWES POINT TO MILSON'S POINT.
Designed by Mr. J. J. C. BRADFIELD.

IC WORKS AND RAILWAYS AND THE OFFICERS DIRECTLY ASSOCIATED WITH
HIM IN THE PASSING OF THE BILL.
RADFIELD, M.E., M.Inst.C.E.; Miss K. M. BUTLER, Confidential Clerk to the Chief Engineer;
Secretary for Public Works; Hon. R. T. BALL, M.L.A., Minister for Public Works and Railways.

The Canadian Bridge Company of Ontario produced two tenders. One followed Bradfield's official cantilever design (except for a system of web bracing that was used in the Quebec Bridge) and while most of the steel would be fabricated in Australia, Bradfield noted that the tender, at £5 313 000, was higher than British tenders for a similar bridge. Their other plan, for an 'inverted

∧ McClintic Marshall Products Co of Pittsburgh tender designs for a cantilever bridge. *Sydney Harbour Bridge: Report on Tenders*, 1924

37

arch' (a stiffened eyebar cable suspension bridge), was cheaper than their cantilever model and Bradfield regarded its appearance as generally pleasing, 'but somewhat marred by the inclined anchorage eyebars beneath the approach spans'. Here again, Bradfield is putting aesthetic appearance on a par with price and strength. His concern for all three factors marks him out as one of the most astute government engineers Australia has ever produced.

Sir William Arrol and Co produced two tenders, both following official designs fairly closely; one for a cantilever bridge and another for an arch bridge. At £4 978 000 and £4 645 000 their quotes were considerably below the preceding tenders. Of the two designs, Bradfield preferred the arch on the grounds that it represented 'one of the highest forms of expression of modern engineering practice'. Indeed, Bradfield was of the opinion that 'the figures for rigidity clearly prove that the arch is by far the most rigid and efficient structure of all three types submitted by tenderers'.

The company to put in the most tenders – seven in all – was Dorman, Long and Co of Middlesbrough, England. They had the notable advantage of having two well-established steel fabricating shops in Australia, one in Sydney and one in Melbourne, and they were already constructing in medium heavy steel of the type required for the approach spans, cross-girders and decking of the Bridge. Bradfield noted approvingly that all their tenders were based 'on the official specifications and plans', and complimented them 'on the excellence of the plans, calculations, and material submitted'. The seven tenders included both cantilever and arch designs, some with abutment towers and some without. Bradfield considered those without to be 'too severe' for their setting, while on another design he thought the abutment towers 'too massive'. Despite the fact

^ An imagined completed arch bridge, illuminated with the insignia of the Australian Imperial Force. 300 000 Australians fought in the Great War, and 60 000 died. State Records New South Wales NRS12685, 1 April 1924

that Bradfield himself had originally favoured a cantilever design, he finally rejected those suggested by Dorman, Long and Co on the grounds that they were 'not as harmonious' as the arch bridge.

After laborious and detailed discussions in which Bradfield had the full resources of the Public Works Department to help with the checking of the calculations and costing, he finally recommended the third of the Dorman Long designs: a two-hinged arch with abutment towers faced with granite masonry, at a cost of £4 217 722. Bradfield admitted that an arch bridge would be harder to build than a suspension or cantilever, but argued that 'with solid rock foreshore [it] is well within the range of present-day knowledge and appliances'. The Dorman Long proposal came with an impeccable pedigree. Its architects were the 'eminent firm' of Sir John Burnet and Partners,

while among its engineers was Ralph Freeman of Sir Douglas Fox and Partners, who had designed the 150-metre span arch bridge across the Zambezi River near Victoria Falls.

Among the specifications for the tenders were a number of requirements about Australian content and the employment of Australian workers. The former had nationalistic appeal for both Labor and non-Labor forces in Parliament, while the latter was particularly appealing to Labor, which may be one reason why they supported the conservative government's Bridge Bill. Clause 16 stated, in part, that 'the contractor must provide in his tender to utilise as far as is reasonably practicable all materials called for by this specification which are being manufactured in New South Wales at the date of the closing of tenders' and as Bradfield commented, 'it is evident that tenderers would obtain a proportion

of their material from the Broken Hill Proprietary Company'. BHP opened Australia's first fully fledged steelworks in Newcastle in 1915. With their workshops in Sydney and Melbourne, Dorman Long, the winning tenderer, were in an excellent position to capitalise on the local materials clause, and of all the tenderers they promised to do by far the highest proportion of their fabrication work in New South Wales.

Although an English firm won the contract, Bradfield pointed out that the Bridge would be wholly fabricated at Milsons Point by 'Australian workmen', that the piers and abutments would be constructed of granite, mined from the south coast town of Moruya, using Nepean River sand and New South Wales cement, and that the Bridge itself would be erected by 'Australian' labour. This was not a provision that bothered Dorman Long because, in negotiating the contract after the tender was accepted, they managed to persuade the New South Wales government to bear the cost of all subsequent wage increases.

Bradfield (as his biographer Richard Raxworthy points out), had no deputy, with the principal design engineers for the Bridge contract, the road approaches and the city railway, all reporting directly to him. Raxworthy writes that Bradfield

> was accessible and moved around the work, checking progress for long hours everyday ... he worked constantly at motivating everybody with personal chats and with official ceremonies [*The Unreasonable Man*, 1989, p 80].

At the conclusion of his *Sydney Harbour Bridge: Report on Tenders* Bradfield wrote:

> Future generations will judge our generation by our works. For that reason and from consideration of the past, I have recommended granite, strong, imperishable, a natural product, rather than a

Illustrations from the McClintic Marshall Products tender document, showing neoclassical pylons in a style popular in the United States at that time. The Dorman Long pylons were built in a much more modern art deco style

cheap artificial material, for the facing of the piers … at times of national rejoicing when the city is illuminated, the arch bridge would be unique in that it could be illuminated to represent the badge of the Australian Commonwealth Military Forces, the sun and crown, a fitting tribute to our soldiers.

When the Bridge finally opened one company called it 'as much a national milestone as Anzac'. Many a company and politician tried to capture the rhetoric that the Bridge made possible: a rhetoric of courage, manliness, self-sufficiency, growth of nationhood and security; the very same characteristics that Australia was said to have developed at Anzac Cove.

The easy passage of the *Harbour Bridge Act*, and the adulatory references to Bradfield which it occasioned, undoubtedly increased his resolve to promote other sections of his scheme. His

promotional campaign had thus far been eminently successful and had encountered remarkably little opposition even from those whose homes stood in the path of his plans. Construction work on the city underground railway helped to further this image, for by mid-1923 the public could see concrete results of the Bradfield plan in the excavation and tunnel building. Bradfield's reputation as an expert received a further fillip in 1924 when he received the Doctorate of Engineering with Honours from the University of Sydney for his thesis entitled 'The City and Suburban Electric Railways and the Sydney Harbour Bridge'. One of his examiners was the famous general and Vice-Chancellor of Melbourne University, Sir John Monash, who wrote that 'these works are undoubtedly of exceptional magnitude, being in some respects unique in Engineering practice'.

∧ By 1925 the Bridge seal had been altered to reflect the change to an arch design. *Ceremony of Setting the Foundation Stone, Dawes Point*, 1925

Clearing approaches: progress and victims

v Dwellings in Princes Street the Rocks, in May 1927, shortly before demolition to make way for the southern approaches to the Bridge. Timber and tin houses, dating from the 1840s, and substantial brick terrace houses from the 1880s, all fell to the demolishers. State Records New South Wales NRS12685, 24 May 1927

Before work could start on the Bridge hundreds of houses and businesses had to be demolished and major changes to the transport system were required on the northern side. When looking at the Bridge approaches today they appear so secure in their landscape that it is hard to imagine that whole swathes of North Sydney and the Rocks were demolished, so the Bridge could take both motor vehicles and trains with ease.

In North Sydney the Milsons Point Station and Ferry Arcade gave way to a new railway station at Lavender Bay, a temporary ferry terminal and a new vehicular ferry at the Jeffrey Street dock. Escalators carried ferry passengers up the cliff face to new tram and bus stops. The changeover from one system to another took just a day. One side of Alfred Street disappeared along with whole sections of Fitzroy, Broughton and Willoughby Streets. On 27 February 1925 the *Sun* reported that 118 houses had already been resumed in North Sydney, with a total of 438 houses to go by the end of the year. With an average occupancy of 4.6, over 2000 people would be displaced. North Sydney Council's response to the problem was simply to note that

the centre of gravity of its population was moving towards its northern boundary.

On 24 June 1926 the *Labor Daily* reported a deputation of waterside workers from Milsons Point who, in Premier Jack Lang's absence in Melbourne, were received by Minister of Justice William McKell. The deputation asked

that provision be made for the housing of some two hundred and forty workers mostly on the water side, who sooner or later, will lose their homes at Milson's Point, owing to bridge resumptions. Introducing the deputation Ald Holdsworth said *they quite recognised that the Bridge was essential, and that progress could not be stayed* [my emphasis].

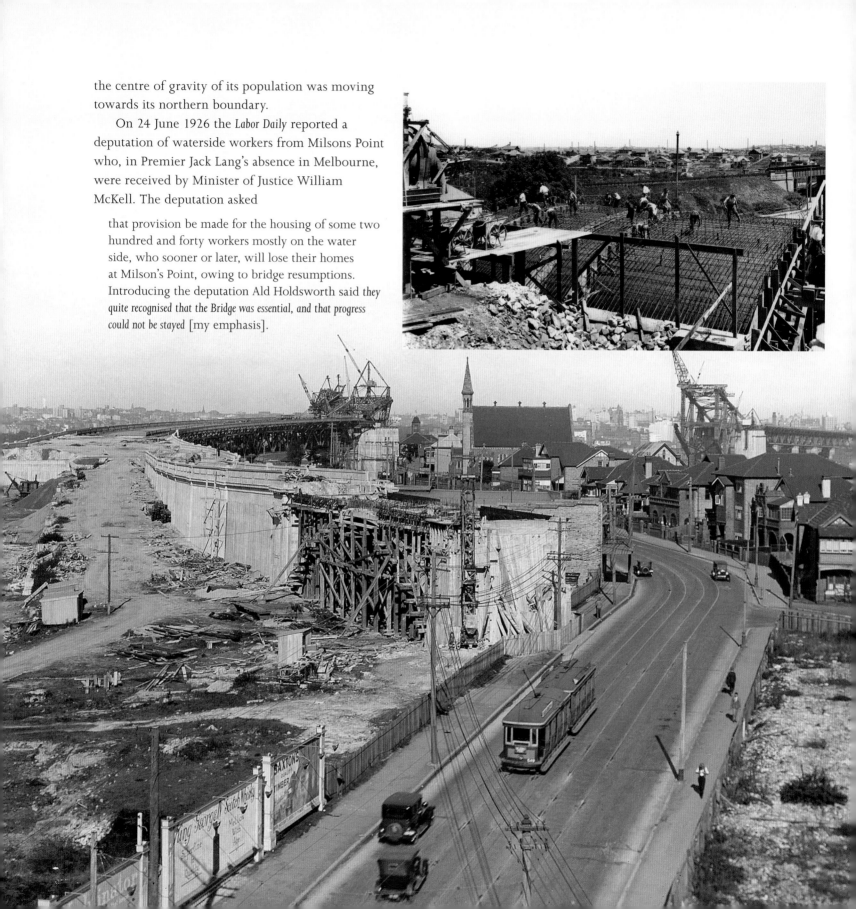

A similar deputation called on McKell from the Rocks. Neither deputation proved militant; in fact, they were remarkably understanding about the Labor government's commitment to the Bradfield plan and to the Bridge in particular. No criticism of Bradfield was implied by the deputation, and he in any case proved co-operative by suggesting a number of possibilities for worker rehousing. McKell said that he would get the government architect onto the matter, but no action was forthcoming.

In a response to the demands of the Milsons Point waterside workers, Premier Lang's advice to cabinet, recorded in a paper of 12 October 1926, noted 'If it is proved that compensation should be given to tenants at will or weekly tenants in North Sydney, then the principle must apply to the whole State.' One of the waterside workers subsequently wrote to the premier that if the money invested in boarding houses and small businesses is to be lost, 'we are to be impoverished to make way for a bridge that is to benefit the property owner' (Peter Lalor, *The Bridge*, 2005, pp 116–17).

At this time the New South Wales Labor government had no State housing authority. The Labor-created Housing Board, which had little to its credit apart from the Daceyville Garden

Suburb near Kensington, was disbanded by a non-Labor government in 1924. During the 1920s the Sydney City Council built a few blocks of flats but none were directly related to the plight of the displaced tenants, nor did that council's jurisdiction extend to North Sydney. McKell was relieved of his undischarged responsibility to rehouse the waterside workers and their families with the defeat of the Labor government in the October 1927 elections, but his failure may well have haunted him. On becoming Labor premier in 1941 one of his first acts was to set up the Housing Commission of New South Wales, whose first large high-rise project after the war was the Greenway Flats built at North Sydney between

< Lawrence Ennis, Chief Construction Engineer for Dorman Long and Co, came from a family of Scottish engineers. He was probably on site more often than any other senior figure, including Bradfield. While supervising construction he lived at the new Astor apartment block in Macquarie St, opened in 1923, which offered a marvellous vantage point for the construction of the Bridge. Caricature by George Finey, *Art in Australia*, June 1931

1949 and 1953 on land left over from the Bridge
construction.

By May 1928, as Daniel Clyne, the Labor
member for the inner-city seat of King, told
Parliament, most of the city-side tenants had
already left. On the south side, Princes Street
disappeared, with its many historic buildings,
as did most of the properties between Princes
Street and Argyle Street. In February 1928 Sydney
Ferries Ltd had claimed £191 000 compensation
for the demolition of its elegant ferry arcade at
Milsons Point. A few months later it managed to
wring £78 000 from the government. Landlords
and businesses received compensation. Displaced
tenants got nothing, other than a government

report by WJ Kessell from the Department of Justice
who noted that businesses and tenants who had
no lease had no rights to compensation, beyond
cartage and expenses, as it would set too great a
precedent.

One of the most revealing commentaries on
the demolition and excavation work came from
the Reverend Frank Cash, rector of Christ Church,
Lavender Bay, North Sydney. A keen photographer,
Cash was refused permission by Bradfield to be on
the site, so instead he got approval from Lawrence
Ennis, director of construction for Dorman Long.
In July 1930 Cash self-published *Parables of the Sydney
Harbour Bridge*, a lavish tome of 534 pages. Ennis
wrote that 'In the preparation of his book he has

been our most constant visitor at the bridge. The men and the staff at the bridge all know him well and have nicknamed him the "Mascot Padre".' Cash presented his record of the construction as a series of parables, an odd mixture of mystical text and documentary commentary.

His sympathy did not extend very far, though he showed some compassion for his parishioners. Of his photograph of a house being demolished in Arthur Street, North Sydney, Cash told his readers that 'the place on which it stood has since been adorned by the building of a beautiful symmetrical concrete arch … when standing in that arch I sometimes hear (in fancy) the crash of this very wall, as it smashed on the ground'.

The biggest and most influential landholder in the way of the Bridge was the Presbyterian Church, taken much more seriously than the displaced tenants. Jack Lang later wrote in his book *I Remember* that

> When the plans for the City Railway and the Harbour Bridge were brought to me in 1925, by Dr JJC Bradfield, he told me that … the historic Presbyterian Scots' Church was situated on the land that had to be resumed for the southern approaches to the Harbour Bridge.

The Lang government, mindful of the political power of the Presbyterian Church and of the need to avoid sectarian strife, readily provided a new site at the corner of Margaret Street and York Street, and a five-storey, sandstone-faced edifice was erected with a handsome government subsidy. Seventy years later it had an apartment tower grafted onto it.

ᵛ The Reverend Frank Cash of Christ Church, Lavender Bay, captured the drama of the demolitions, the precursor to his photographs of Bridge building, documented in his book *Parables of Sydney Harbour Bridge*, 1930

^ One of the many shops
demolished to make way
for the Bridge approaches.
Unless they held freehold
land, neither businesses
nor residents were offered
compensation
by the State government.
Corner of Kent and
Crescent Streets. State
Records New South Wales
NRS12685, May 1927

North Shore Bridge

Not content with the enormous program of suburban electrification (including the Hornsby–Milsons Point, Homebush, Granville–Liverpool and Lidcombe–Cabramatta lines), Bradfield began to advocate for his projected railway lines from Sydney to St Leonards and Eastwood, and from Sydney to Mosman and Manly.

> The city proper will become a New York in miniature whilst North Sydney, Mosman and Willoughby will merge into a second Brooklyn, with property values in places equalling those of the city. The districts of Lane Cove, Ku-ring-gai and Hornsby … will become most sought after as residential suburbs, and will carry a large population, living in ideal and healthy surroundings.

Such sentiments, and particularly the analogy of New York, which in the 1920s had become Hollywood's symbol of urban progress, established Bradfield as one of the key metropolitan boosters of his time, while his well-known advocacy for residential development in the healthy suburbs may be partly attributed to the fact that like an increasing proportion of Sydney's professional class he himself resided there, in his case at leafy Gordon, halfway up the North Shore line.

Bradfield's pronouncements about the role of the Bridge in suburban residential expansion became so well-known that in December 1927, five years before completion, a half-page real estate advertisement in the *Herald* was created around them. The advertisement told of a projected 'Garden Suburb' at Narrabeen, to be developed by 'the eminent architect, engineer and town planner', Norman Weekes, an acquaintance of Bradfield's in the Town Planning Association.

∧ Arthur Rickard and Co were Sydney's most imaginative real estate developers and advertisers. This advertisement, placed some months after the Wall Street crash, appealed to both investors and owner occupiers. *Daily Guardian*, 9 July 1930.
> The drawings, including p. 46, are from *The Bridge Book, Art in Australia*, 1930

< The railway, tramway and ferry terminus at Lavender Bay was opened in July 1924 to replace the terminus at Milsons Point, demolished to make way for the northern Bridge approaches. *Ceremony of Setting the Foundation Stone at Dawes Point*, 1925

v Built in England in 1930–31, the P&O liner *Strathaird*, visited Sydney in 1932. The British designer of this jigsaw depicted the Bridge from the western side with the Dorman Long workshops replaced by a green verge (where Luna Park and the North Sydney Pool now stand). Cardboard jigsaw box, 1931, Spearritt collection

Twelve months ago Dr Bradfield told the Sydney Press that the future would be a period of unprecedented development for the Northern Suburbs; that within the next twenty years the unimproved capital value of North Shore property will exceed that of the city, and that this will be mainly due to the fact that the bridge will afford the Northern Suburbs adequate road and railway communication with the city. As a result of the Bridge, Dr Bradfield concluded, it has been estimated that the population of the Northern Suburbs will be at least 290,000 in 1931, which will be double what it was in 1921.

No one doubted the popularity of the Bridge with the burgesses of the North Shore, least of all themselves. Indeed, until the late 1920s it was still in popular parlance referred to as

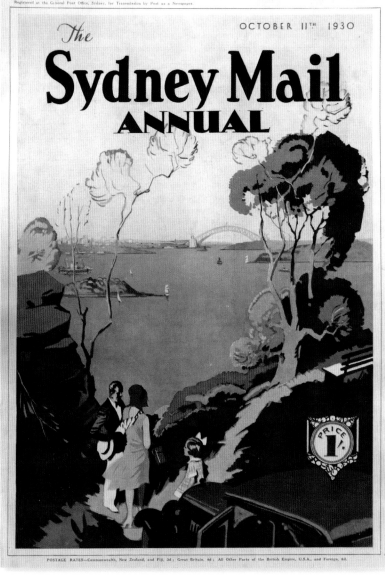

^ Arthur Rickard and Co used the promise of the Bridge and the new suburban electric trains to convince home owners and investors that distant Roseville was readily accessible to the city centre. *Daily Guardian*, 20 May 1930

^ A patrician North Shore family have motored to North Head to admire the distant Bridge under construction, offering the middle class direct automobile access to the city. The Bridge arch has been completed, but the pylons are still under construction and the bridge deck is yet to come. Front cover, *Sydney Mail Annual*, October 1930

the 'North Shore Bridge', despite the fact that in official circles it had been called the 'Sydney Harbour Bridge' since the passing of the enabling act in 1922. Writing a series of articles for the *Herald* on 'A Growing City', a North Shore gentleman told his readers in 1927 that 'The North Shore lives for its great bridge', which it needed to overcome 'the inconveniences and disabilities which attend the lives of those who

have gone to live in the Valhalla north of the city' with 'more attractive houses to the square mile than any other part of Sydney'. Three years later, the Reverend Frank Cash wrote in his photo commentary upon the demolitions for the Bridge:

The windowless terrace is representative of old North Shore; the arch of beautiful symmetry is representative of a vigorous, growing city, on the north side of the Harbour.

The arch that cut the skies

It 'appened this way: I'ad jist come down,
After long years, to look at Sydney town,
An' struth! Was I knocked endways? Fair suprised?
I never dreamed! That arch that cut the skies!

When CJ Dennis wrote his hymn of praise, 'I Dips me Lid to the Sydney Harbour Bridge', Sydneysiders had lived with the excitement of construction for seven years. The successful tenderer was announced to an expectant public in March 1924 and from that day onward hardly a week went by in which the Sydney press did not carry some item or feature article on the Bridge. The Fairfax-owned *Sydney Mail* had already commissioned a series of articles on the Bridge by Bradfield's secretary, Kathleen M Butler, ten of which appeared before the successful tenderer was announced and another 17 after. Once excavations began in January 1925 most of these articles were illustrated with graphic photographs of preparations for the approaches and later of the growing structure itself.

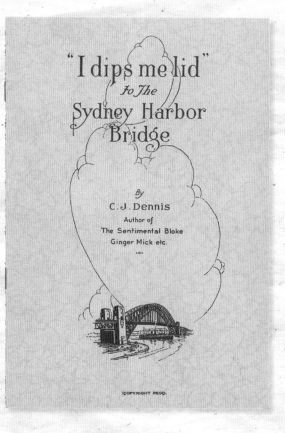

"I dips me lid" to The Sydney Harbor Bridge

By C. J. Dennis
Author of The Sentimental Bloke Ginger Mick etc.

(COPYRIGHT REGD.)

Once Dorman Long's tender at £4 217 722 had been accepted, the company had to set about putting its plans into operation. Two days after signing the contract in Sydney, Lawrence Ennis set out for London by sea. Commercial flights between Australia and London were not inaugurated till the mid-1930s and the sea journey took six weeks. Given the frequent movement of key Dorman Long personnel between Sydney and London, the speed with which the Bridge was constructed (seven years from the start of excavations in January 1925) is remarkable. In contrast, the Sydney Opera House, which quickly fell prey to design and cost controversies, took well over a decade to build.

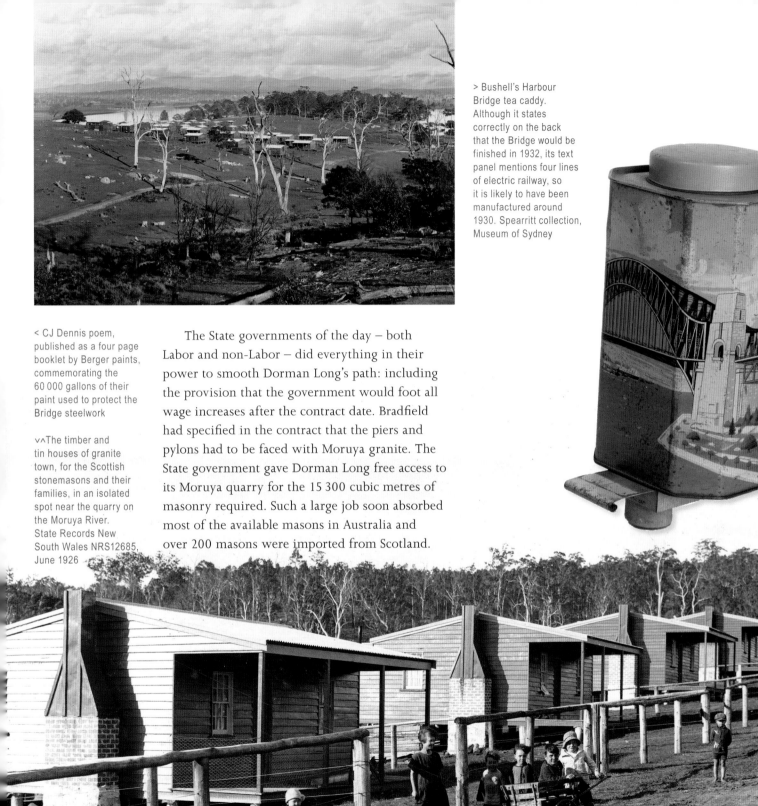

> Bushell's Harbour Bridge tea caddy. Although it states correctly on the back that the Bridge would be finished in 1932, its text panel mentions four lines of electric railway, so it is likely to have been manufactured around 1930. Spearritt collection, Museum of Sydney

< CJ Dennis poem, published as a four page booklet by Berger paints, commemorating the 60 000 gallons of their paint used to protect the Bridge steelwork

∨∧The timber and tin houses of granite town, for the Scottish stonemasons and their families, in an isolated spot near the quarry on the Moruya River. State Records New South Wales NRS12685, June 1926

The State governments of the day – both Labor and non-Labor – did everything in their power to smooth Dorman Long's path: including the provision that the government would foot all wage increases after the contract date. Bradfield had specified in the contract that the piers and pylons had to be faced with Moruya granite. The State government gave Dorman Long free access to its Moruya quarry for the 15 300 cubic metres of masonry required. Such a large job soon absorbed most of the available masons in Australia and over 200 masons were imported from Scotland.

With a population just over 1000, Moruya could not cope with such an influx so in 1925, in the best traditions of corporate paternalism, the company provided 72 wooden cottages for the 250 workers and their families, along with a village store, post office and social hall. The Education Department provided a school and the settlement soon earned the nickname 'Granite Town'.

The contract also provided for most of the fabrication work to be done locally. The State government therefore provided Dorman Long with a large site on the northern side of the harbour with a waterfrontage adjacent to the Bridge. Today the site is occupied by the North Sydney Municipal Swimming Pool (1936) and Luna Park (1935). A total of 42 000 cubic metres of rock and earth had to be excavated before the Bridge fabrication shops could be erected. A wharf large enough to receive overseas vessels was built adjacent to the workshops and at the finishing end a dock was constructed so that barges could take delivery of completed members from the shop cranes.

Activity in the three sections of the fabrication shops went on day and night. The scene, as film taken at the time suggests, was akin to what one would see in a medium-sized steel foundry. The fabrication shops had a 'loght' section with four cranes, each of 25-tonnes capacity, a 'template' section, and a 'heavy' section with two cranes, each of 122-tonnes capacity. Looking at the settled image that the Bridge represents today, it is hard to imagine the bustle of construction activity in Lavender Bay which lasted for seven years.

At that time Lavender Bay and much of North Sydney housed a predominantly working-class population of tenants, so the industrial activity associated with the Bridge was not as novel or as unexpected as it would be to the middle-class residents of today. North Sydney housed a number of small factories, while just along the harbour foreshores sawmilling was an important industry along with the North Shore Gas Company's installation near Balls Head (named after the Minister for Public Works who had presided over the *Bridge Act's* passage through Parliament).

The wharf and dock for the Bridge fabrication workshops received a constant stream of ships. Once berthed, the ship's material – much of which came from Dorman Long's Middlesbrough Works in England – was unloaded by wharf cranes and transferred to the stockyard cranes. The steel was then straightened and cut to the correct length and width. In the words of the Director of Construction, Lawrence Ennis:

> Although, on completion, the arch presents to the sight a perfect curve, it is built up on straight members, the effect of the curve in the completed structure being given by bevels machined at the butt joints of bottom and top chord members.

∧ Kandos cement, befitting a local New South Wales firm, were keen to claim credit for supporting 'entirely' the Bridge, although the pylons above the deck level are purely decorative. *Australasian Engineer,* March 1932

Building the approaches

By September 1926 concrete piers had been built to support the approach spans on either side of the harbour. Two lines of timber 'falsework' supported the approach span steelwork as it moved from pier to pier. A 25-tonne crane was erected on each timber tower and travelled forwards on the steelwork which it had placed in position; that is, the cranes built their own track as they moved along the approaches.

While the approach spans were being erected on either side of the harbour, excavations proceeded for the base of the main pylons and the 'skewback' foundations. The skewbacks, enormous concrete footings 12-metres deep, took the thrust of the main arch below the main bearings at an angle of 45 degrees. The four bearings, each weighing 330 tonnes, were manufactured in England. They were placed in sections on a steel framework which was later removed, and after being adjusted with the aid of hydraulic jacks, they were concreted from the underside.

At this stage the pylons were also taking shape. The construction of the two huge abutments on either side of the harbour was necessary both to support the approaching spans and to provide a foundation for the main

∨ Tunneling under Bank Street, North Sydney, with both trucks and horse-drawn carts taking away the rubble. Both the workers and the two schoolboys are conscious that a photograph is being taken. State Records New South Wales NRS12685, March 1924

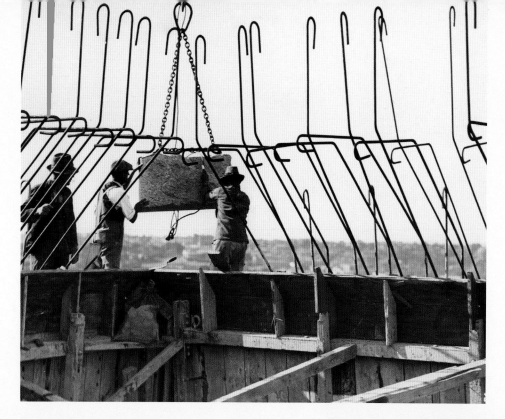

bearings. The pylons themselves are merely architectural decoration, an aspect of the Bridge's construction that it is often commented upon. Bradfield had included them in his specifications for the tenderers because of his view that a bridge which lacked pylons would look too severe and an uninformed public might otherwise wonder about its stability.

By June 1928 the five approach spans on each side of the harbour 'stood out on the skyline upon their granite piers'. Today the grassed areas abutting the approaches are a favourite spot for picnickers on both sides of the harbour, but of course during the construction the entire Bridge site was out of bounds except to the select few who had sufficient political or professional clout to be taken on a tour of inspection. The Reverend Frank Cash seems to have been the only 'outsider' with regular access to the site. In this respect the construction of the Bridge was quite different

56

from that of many other public buildings, such as the Sydney Opera House, where the government of the day was so anxious to convince the public of money well spent that tours were not only permitted but encouraged. Souvenir hunters at the Opera House (including myself as a teenager) were placated by being allowed to carry off cracked and discarded tiles originally intended for the sails.

ᵛ Stages of construction from September 1927 to September 1931, showing the half arches, supported by steel cables in bedrock, through to the closing of the arch and the hanging of the deck. *The Story of Sydney Harbour Bridge*, Department of Main Roads, 1980

∧ The Western railway track through a pylon tower. The art deco lights for the pedestrian/cycleway are clearly visible. State Records New South Wales NRS12685, January 1932

< Pouring concrete into the Fitzroy Street arch at Milsons Point in June 1928. In a pre hard-hat era, all but one of the workmen are wearing felt hats or cloth caps. State Records New South Wales NRS12685, 1928

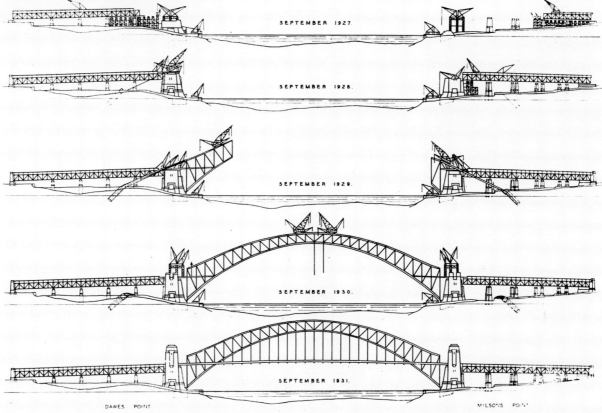

SEPTEMBER 1927.

SEPTEMBER 1928.

SEPTEMBER 1929.

SEPTEMBER 1930.

SEPTEMBER 1931.

DAWES POINT   MILSONS POINT

<^v The cable tunnel saddle being prepared in July 1928 with cables inserted by June 1929. State Records New South Wales NRS12685. The diagram shows the steel cables embedded in the cable saddles. WJ Watson, *A Decade of Bridges*, 1937

^ The arches in June 1930, taken from the West Rocks. The cables holding back the top chords are clearly shown, as are the creeper cranes. The pylons have been completed to deck level. Erection Wages photo album, 1932

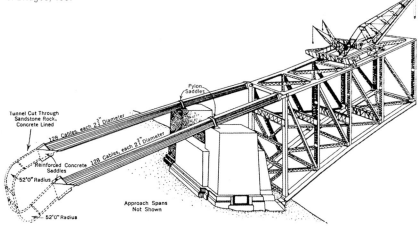

Erecting the arches

Public interest in the Bridge increased a hundredfold as work began on the construction of the arches. Up to that point it had looked much like any other engineering project, with preparation not unlike the excavation for the city railway stations of Museum and St James, opened in December 1926, for which most of Hyde Park was cut up at one time or another. Building the arches made all the difference.

Between June 1928 and August 1930, when the Bridge arches finally met, newspapers drew the public's attention almost daily to the progress of the 'giant span' (a favourite phrase among journalists at the time). The Bridge had already proved a boon to newspapers and magazines short of copy, but the construction of the arches was so much more spectacular than anything that had gone before that

∧ *The Bridge Book*, Art in Australia, 1930

∨ Aerial photograph of the half arches taken from above McMahons Point, late 1929. State Records New South Wales NRS 12685

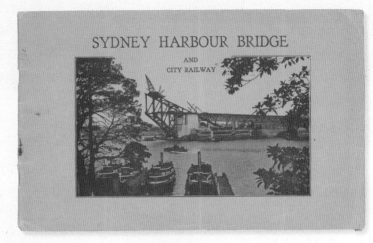

∧ Commemorative booklet published in Sydney in 1927

press, amateur and professional photographers vied to shoot the Bridge from a new angle or in a new light. The slowly growing arches provided a ready-made motif for cartoonists to moralise upon and avant-garde painters to experiment with.

As the arches grew, Sydneysiders no longer had to rely on the press or a visit to 'town' to see the progress of their bridge. Increasingly the structure itself could be seen from many vantage points around the city. From high points near the National Park in the south, Bankstown and Ashfield in the southwest, Epping to the north and Vaucluse to the east, the two sides of the arch could be seen reaching out across the harbour. To those who travelled to work in or near the city centre by ferry, whether from Parramatta at the western extension of the harbour or Manly to the northeast, the progress of the Bridge became part of every working day. On weekends and during

school holidays children going from Circular Quay to Taronga Zoo got a spectacular view of the arches being built.

The late 1920s was the period of peak patronage for Sydney's ferry system, which carried 47 million passengers in 1927 and 43 million in a more depressed 1931. In the absence of a main harbour crossing, all train passengers had to alight at Milsons Point Station and catch a ferry, as did tram passengers from the northern suburbs system, though they also had the choice of alighting at Athol Wharf by Taronga Zoo or at the ferry wharves in Mosman, Cremorne and Neutral Bay. Those select members of the middle class who could afford their own cars used the vehicular ferries.

> Hundreds of businesses attempted to cash in on the Bridge, from those directly related to the construction to real estate agents and manufacturers of any and every product. Here a toothpaste manufacturer has produced a tin advertising sign, c 1928. Spearritt collection, Museum of Sydney

∨ As the arches crept out over the harbour they presented a stunning sight, photographed here from Lavender Bay. State Records New South Wales NRS12685, May 1930

Sydney Harbour Bridge

∧ The half arches reaching out on both sides of the harbour could be seen from near and far. Spearritt collection, 1930

The technical details of erecting the arches were explained in well-illustrated and laborious detail in the popular press. No Sydney newspaper, no matter how parochial, chose to ignore the ever-growing structure. Even the distant *Cumberland Argus and Fruitgrowers' Advocate*, based in Parramatta, carried pictures of its growth. The Bridge became the greatest symbol of engineering prowess that Australia had ever known: a symbol of 'Man's power' over his environment. Engineering feats were then – as they are still depicted today – the preserve of men.

The arch was cantilevered out from either side of the harbour using steel wire cables to anchor back the half-arches until they met in the centre to be joined by a horizontal bearing pin, thereby becoming self-supporting. This method of construction, where the foundation and abutments had to withstand the 'pull' of the half-arch and the weight of the 574-tonne 'creeper cranes', might not have been possible had the harbour foreshores not been composed of solid sandstone. The creeper cranes, one to straddle the arch at the northern side and one at the southern, were actually erected *in situ* by the 25-tonne cranes which had been used to construct the approach spans. The main hoist of each creeper crane had a lifting capacity of 124 tonnes.

The creeper cranes began by erecting the first panel of the arch and then crept forward from panel to panel, building as they went. During erection, the individual half-arches were anchored back by 128 special steel-wire cables, manufactured in England. The wires were secured in horseshoe-shaped anchorage tunnels, excavated in solid rock to a depth of 40 metres. Though each cable had a breaking stress of 467 tonnes, they were never called upon to sustain a strain of more than 117 tonnes. This preoccupation with

∨ The southern arch in May 1930, showing the two sets of cables holding back the top chords. State Records New South Wales NRS12685

engineering surety was typical of all aspects of the construction of the Bridge, and formed a marked contrast to Dorman Long's cavalier attitude to the safety of the Bridge workers themselves.

The technological ingenuity which went into the Bridge should not be underestimated, and unlike more modern bridges, most of this ingenuity had to be exercised on the site. Assembly and disassembly of the construction units, especially the cranes, was a constant feature. The whole construction process was much easier for the general public to understand than modern bridge technology, which relies so much on the

qualities of cement and aerodynamics. Anyone reading a newspaper and taking an occasional look themselves could understand the role of the component parts. Children experimented with their very own Meccano Bridges. Sporting stores displayed scale models to entice customers.

On 26 October 1928 the 40-metre tunnels, erected simultaneously with the abutments, were ready to receive the cables. After completion of the first part of the arch (including top and bottom chords, diagonals, panel posts and bracing) the creeper cranes were in a position to make their slow trek out over the harbour. Once the nose of each side of the arch projected over the harbour the steel had to be lifted from a barge in mid-stream, an operation demanding considerable care because the harbour had to be open at all times to ferry and shipping traffic. Had a bridge design with mid-harbour columns been adopted, not only would taller ships have been prevented from sailing to the wharves beyond Circular Quay, but commerce and passenger traffic on the harbour would have been severely curtailed during construction. Such harbour traffic was much more frequent than it is today when containerisation, including the establishment of Port Botany in the 1970s, much larger ships and air freight have dramatically reduced the number of vessels entering and leaving the harbour. To ensure the safety of ferry passengers and general shipping, all crane movements were controlled by a telephone link from the barges to the crane cabs 137 metres above.

SYDNEY HARBOUR BRIDGE

> Hand drawn figures from *The Bridge Book*, Art in Australia, 1930

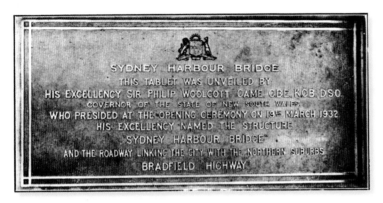

SYDNEY HARBOUR BRIDGE
THIS TABLET WAS UNVEILED BY
HIS EXCELLENCY SIR PHILIP WOOLCOTT GAME, G.B.E., K.C.B., D.S.O.
GOVERNOR OF THE STATE OF NEW SOUTH WALES,
WHO PRESIDED AT THE OPENING CEREMONY ON 19TH MARCH 1932.
HIS EXCELLENCY NAMED THE STRUCTURE
"SYDNEY HARBOUR BRIDGE"
AND THE ROADWAY LINKING THE CITY WITH THE NORTHERN SUBURBS
BRADFIELD HIGHWAY

∧ These carefully worded plaques can still be seen on the eastern Bridge walkway and on the south-eastern pylon

Who really designed the Bridge?

In 1929, when the two halves of the arch were making their slow but certain creep across the harbour, controversy flared between the two men who could claim primary credit for the design of the Bridge. A series of articles appeared in the *Sydney Morning Herald* by Ralph Freeman, the British consulting engineer to Dorman Long, who was described by the *Herald* as 'the designer' of the Bridge and who conveyed the same impression in his articles. The *Herald* took the view that Freeman and not Bradfield was responsible for the design, on the grounds that he had prepared most of the technical drawings. Ball, now Minister for Lands, said it was really difficult to determine what was really meant by the term 'designer'; he would describe the Bridge as a Bradfield–Dorman Long design. EA Buttenshaw, Secretary for Public Works, called for a report on the matter from

Bradfield, who wrote, 'I originated the cantilever bridge design recommended by the public works committee in 1913 and subsequently the arch bridge design of 1650 feet span.' He went on to say that Freeman was not the designer and that tenders were called on his own design. The controversy was never finally resolved, but when Bradfield retired in 1933, the Director of Public Works stated that Bradfield was the designer of the Bridge and that 'no other person by any stretch of imagination, can claim that distinction'. However, modifications had been made to the design after Freeman's visit in 1926, and in 1932 Dorman Long threatened to sue the government if it erected a plaque naming Bradfield as the designer. The Institute of Engineers had already directed that Bradfield and Freeman desist from their public spat, to maintain the dignity of the profession. The plaque finally erected by the government credits both Bradfield and Freeman.

< Caricature of Ralph Freeman, the consulting engineer for Dorman Long, who 'has just arrived in Sydney to watch the Harbour Bridge make ends meet'. On 9 August 1930 *Smith's Weekly* poetically urged Bradfield and Freeman to 'cease these words … Compose those warring faces … Nor trump each other's aces'. Line drawing from *The Bridge Book, Art in Australia*, 1930

Closing the arch

The excitement and anticipation felt by all as the two parts of the arch grew out to meet each other is summed up in the July 1930 issue of the railway and tramway journal *The Staff*:

> Interest in the great bridge which will span Sydney Harbour … is increasing as the structure rears its head into view of many parts of the city and suburbs and the higher lands further out. Surprise at its great size has been general.

As the part-arches reached over the harbour the cables were 'tensioned' to allow for the increasing weight of the structure they were holding back. With the bottom chord all but completed, the gap at the centre was 1.07 metres. The director of construction later wrote that 'A severe gale was experienced when the structure was in this condition, and it was an impressive sight to stand on the forward end of one 825-foot arm and see the

swaying end of the other arm. Indicators, however, registered that the total movement between the two arms was barely 3 inches.' Ennis went on to describe the closure:

> The first closure was effected at 4:15 pm in the afternoon of the 19th August 1930, but there was a subsequent slight opening with the contraction in the cool of the evening. Slacking of the cables was continued without intermission, and the final closure was made at 10 pm the same day. Next morning the Union Jack was flown from the jib of one creeper crane, and the Australian Ensign from the other, to signify to the City that the arch had successfully closed. We felt that the arch had become not only a link between the two shores of a beautiful Harbour, but a further bond of Empire.

And it was as a 'bond of Empire', in the best traditions of British imperialism, that Dorman Long

∧ Lawrence Ennis, the largest figure in the group, supervising preparatioins for the closing of the bottom chord on 13 August 1930. One worker heats up a rivet while another is banging one into place. Erection Wages photo album, 1932

liked to depict the Bridge. In the frenzy of self-congratulation that accompanied the opening 19 months later, much was made of this bond, with most of the British press hailing the Bridge as a 'triumph of British Engineering'. That Australians had thought up the idea, raised the loan funds, manufactured some of the materials and physically erected the structure was all too readily forgotten, though at that time many Australians still thought of themselves as British, even if they were born locally.

Once the bottom chord of the arch was closed the cables were removed and coiled. The closure of the upper chord was not so dramatic, though equally ticklish from the engineers' point of view. Freeman, fresh for his public controversy with Bradfield, travelled from London to Sydney in 1930 to direct the two closures, and the top chord was finally closed on 8 September 1930. Before closure the opposing members of the chord were forced apart so that each side would bear an equal share

of the weight. The great arch, whose progress Sydneysiders had watched with bated breath for almost two years, was finally complete. Advertisers and iconoclastic cartoonists were presented with a symbol worth capturing. The temptation to suggest that it might collapse was too great for some to resist. As the Sydney litterateur Leon Gellert saw it:

The Great Arch of the Sydney Harbour Bridge is complete. For seven years millions of people have awaited this event, many with apprehension, not a few with feelings of misgivings. For five years ferry-boat passengers have scrambled for those positions on deck from which its tremendous proportions might best be seen. Each day, coming and going across their strip of water, they have lifted their eyes to that web of iron in the sky … The two creeping cranes, each on the crest of its own arc, like stupendous and purposeful spiders busy with warp and weft, have at last met over the water.

˅ The western side of the centre joint on the top chord, with a riveter holding his mallet high above the harbour. State Records New South Wales NRS12685, 3 September 1930

< Bradfield, Ellis and Davison, the Minister for Public Works, on a temporary wooden walkway abutting the steel chords. State Records New South Wales NRS12685, 17 February 1931

The CENTRE PIN

< 'Celebration'. This photograph by Cazneaux shows the Union Jack and the Australian flag flying from the creeper cranes, with aircraft saluting the joining of the bottom chord. *The Bridge Book, Art in Australia, 1930*

^ 'Up to this point, both sections were temporarily supported by scores of immensely strong steel wire cables anchored through tunnels in the solid rock; but since the sections have met in the centre, the completed arch requires no external support. Where each half came to rest against the other, the weight was taken by the Centre pin. Vaccum Oil brochure, Sydney 1930. Spearritt collection

The bottom chord, photographed by John Storey from Dawes Point in September 2006

∧ By December 1930
hanging the deck was
well underway. This
photograph, from
Milsons Point, shows the
enormous quantity of
steel parts at the Dorman
Long workshops, most of
which were hauled up by
the creeper crane drivers
from barges below. State
Records New South
Wales NRS12685

Hanging the deck

Once the two half-arches had been joined, the arch
itself became a three-hinged structure, the main
bearing pins at the base constituting two of the
hinges, and the bearing pin at the centre the third.
As with the arch, erecting the hangers posed strategic
problems but these were overcome by the development of a cradle which lifted the hangers one by one
into a horizontal position once they had cleared the
barge. The hangers, with a maximum height of 59
metres, were erected on either side of the arch.

Erection of the hangers and the deck proceeded
much more rapidly than the building of the
approach spans and the arch. Within nine months
of completing the arch, the deck – including
hangers, cross girders, bracing, railway and
roadway stringers and pressed plates – was finished.
The roadway was then concreted and asphalted.
Railway and tramway overhead wiring supports
were quickly added, along with ironbark sleepers
for the railway tracks. Simultaneously, the pylon
towers were concreted and granite-faced from the

69

< The half completed deck. As the narrator in the Harrington Limited film put it, 'piece by piece, like a huge Meccano set, the deck takes shape'.
P Spearritt, *The Sydney Harbour Bridge: a life*, Sydney 1982

Moruya quarries to their final height of 87 metres. In a city where buildings were not allowed to reach above 150 feet (46 metres) the pylons, like the arch itself, towered above the surrounding landscape.

Responsibility for supervising the construction of the Bridge on behalf of the New South Wales government lay with Dr Bradfield, who since 1913 had been Chief Engineer for Metropolitan Railway Construction. Bradfield was also responsible for testing the structure for safety. But in February 1930 Bradfield fell out with his employers, the Railway Commissioners, who curtly retired him from his post. Bradfield had planned the suburban electrification but he had not been responsible for the work. The Railway Commissioners were always trying to get Bradfield to economise on both the Bridge and the city railway. In an unusual move, almost certainly reflecting the elevated position Bradfield held in the eyes of the community, Premier Bavin's Cabinet preserved his status in the Department of Public Works and his £3000 salary, and he continued to represent the government in dealings with the contractors and to supervise construction of the Bridge.

∧ Seeing the Bridge built was like being in on a Meccano set construction, but on a grand scale. The daily press explained the process to Sydneysiders at every step along the way. The publishers of souvenir brochures about Sydney were keen to emphasise not only the reality of construction but the romance of the finished product, here depicted by moonlight. Such images appeared in a number of brochures in the 1930s including *The Part Played by British General Electric Co Ltd*, 1932, Spearritt collection

The battle of the bridges

In the 1920s, New York, the most populous American city, embarked on a huge bridge building program to cater for the rapid rise in motor vehicle usage. As the world's first car owning democracy, the demand for bridges and tunnels to link Manhattan Island with the New York boroughs and to link Staten Island to New Jersey, saw a plethora of tunnels and bridges built in the 1920s and 1930s.

When the contract was signed for the Bayonne Bridge, between Staten Island and New Jersey, over the Kill van Kull river in July 1928, work had been underway on the Sydney Harbour Bridge for five years. The Bayonne Bridge, overseen by the New York Port Authority, had to have 150 feet clearance because the shipping channel it crossed carried more tonnage than the Suez Canal. Having full access to all the details and plans of the Sydney Harbour Bridge the Port Authority decided to make its Kill van Kull Bridge, as it was then called, two feet, one inch longer. In its 1930 report on the progress of construction, where it bragged that the Bayonne Bridge would be finished before the Sydney Bridge, it listed the other large arch bridges in the world, including the Eads Bridge, St Louis (1874, 520 feet), the Niagara Bridge at Niagara Falls (1898, 840 feet) the Hell Gate Bridge, New York (1916, 977 feet), the Sydney Harbour Bridge (1650 feet) and the Bayonne Bridge (1652 feet, 1 inch).

Although 25 inches longer, the Bayonne Bridge, as a cost cutting measure, opened with just four lanes of vehicular roadway, 40 feet between curbs, and a western sidewalk, outside of the arch truss. Provision

HELL GATE BRIDGE, NEW YORK CITY   3A-H1278

In the first four decades of the 20th century the United States and New York in particular became the centre of world bridge construction, following on from the 19th century achievements of British engineers. The Hell Gate Bridge (1916) came at the end of the great era of railroad bridge building, while the Triborough (1936) and Bayonne (1931) bridges, under the supervision of Othmar Ammann, heralded the arrival of mass car ownership, as they were only road bridges without rail or trams. Postcards late 1930s, Spearritt collection

TRIBOROUGH AND HELL-GATE BRIDGES OVER EAST RIVER, NEW YORK CITY   40

K4834

SYDNEY BRIDGE 1,650 FT. SPAN

HELL GATE, NEW YORK, LARGEST
ARCH BRIDGE IN WORLD — 1000 FT. SPAN.

< All the Australian and British accounts of the Bridge were keen to claim it as the largest in the world, which it was in weight and width, but not the longest span, hence the local preference to compare it with the Hell Gate Bridge rather than the Bayonne Bridge. Spearritt collection

least, acknowledge its length. The opening, understandably, made the front page of the *New York Times*. In contrast to the extraordinary parochialism of the Sydney press, the *New York Times* reported that the Sydney Harbour Bridge would be twice as heavy as the Bayonne, and therefore 'larger' but not longer. The New York Port Authority gave the Secretary for Australia in the United States a pair of inscribed gold shears to be sent to Premier Lang for the opening in Sydney. The blades were then to be separated, one to be kept in Australia and the other returned to New York.

< A Moruya granite block being put in place on one of the pylon parapets with both Ennis and Bradfield looking on. State Records New South Wales NRS 12685

was made for the roadway to be widened to seven lanes or take two rapid transit tracks. This never happened, and even today the average daily use at 20 000 vehicles is just one eighth of the motor vehicle traffic across the Sydney Bridge.

When the Bayonne Bridge opened on 15 November 1931, the Sydney press ignored it. The *Sydney Morning Herald* devoted a mere two sentences to the opening in its 'Cable News', neglecting to mention that the Bayonne was longer than the Sydney Bridge. The Melbourne *Age* did, at

29 — AIRPLANE VIEW OF THE TRIBOROUGH AND HELL GATE BRIDGES, NEW YORK CITY

Photo © International News

BAYONNE BRIDGE, NEW YORK CITY

The Bayonne Bridge never developed the symbolic power of the Sydney Harbour Bridge. As just one of many great bridges in New York, it lacked the dramatic setting of the most famous bridges, including the Brooklyn Bridge. By the 1950s the industrial areas that the Bayonne joined were in a state of decay. Today, the Bayonne Bridge itself is in a state of decay, badly rusted and with only minimal maintenance to maintain the roadway.

On 12 January 1932 the contractors handed the Sydney Harbour Bridge to the Department of Public Works for tests, under the supervision of Dr Bradfield. The most spectacular tests took place in early February when 92 locomotives, weighing over 8300 tonnes, were shunted onto the Bridge back to back to test the arch. Engineers knew it would stand up, but the display of locomotives was proof positive for the general public, and

another press opportunity for Bradfield. Soon there would be no reminders of the years of frenzied activity, for as the *Herald* commented but three weeks after the opening:

The largest bridge fabricating shops in the Empire, capable of employing more than 2000 men a day in three shifts, worked incessantly. Every few minutes ferries drew into the wharf, disgorged their human cargo, and departed full again, for Circular Quay … Cargo steamers with granite or steel, or machinery, berthed beside the workshops. Foremen's whistles blew … Today? Ferry journeys from the Quay to 'The Point' already are but a memory. So is the hive of activity that was the workshops. And the giant crane, slowly, relentlessly, continues to eat its way through the remains of the workshops, and the gloomy workmen pack away the ruin that it leaves behind [9 April 1932].

SYDNEY HARBOUR BRIDGE
MARCH 19TH 1932
LENGTH OF BRIDGE AND APPROACHES 2 MILES 33 CHAINS
WIDTH OF DECK 159 FEET 11 INCHES

73

The opening

On completion of the Bridge deck, public attention turned to plans for the opening ceremonies. Government departments and private industry had been debating for some time about the form the opening should take and the amount that should be spent on it.

On 30 May 1931 the Premier's Department wrote to the Director of Public Works to inform him that Saturday 19 March 1932 had been set aside as the opening day. It is an indication of how seriously the government took the opening that it then declared this a public holiday. (Very many people – not only shop assistants – still worked a half day on Saturday.) The Premier's Department went on to stress that it was not the government's intention 'to expend some thousands of pounds at such a time of financial depression in the extension of an invitation to Royalty to perform the Opening Ceremony, but it would probably adopt a suggestion that His Majesty should be asked to do so, by wireless'. Labor Premier Jack Lang refused to bow to subsequent demands from the paramilitary, right-wing New Guard to get royalty to open the Bridge. A Sydney Harbour Bridge Celebrations Committee, set up by leading citizens in June 1931, aimed to raise money and business interest in the celebrations. Presided over by Joseph Jackson, the non-Labor Lord Mayor of Sydney, it included leading city retailers, Sir Samuel Hordern and Charles Lloyd Jones and the theatrical entrepreneur EJ Tait. That a number of Labor MLAs agreed to serve on a business-dominated committee is indicative of the bipartisan approval of the Bridge. Not surprisingly Bradfield agreed to serve on the committee. It soon produced a lavish letterhead reflecting its aim to promote Sydney both nationally and internationally. Superimposed on a striking colour poster of a manly Australian surf lifesaver, with the

SOUVENIR

COMMONWEALTH OF AUSTRALIA
Postmaster-General's Department.

TELEGRAM

SYDNEY HARBOUR BRIDGE

LOCATION:
DAWES POINT TO MILSONS POINT,
SYDNEY.
Chief Engineer:
J.J.C.BRADFIELD,
D.Sc.Eng., M.E., M.Inst. C.E., M.I.E.Aust.
Contractors for the main bridge:
DORMAN, LONG & COY, LTD.
Middlesbrough & London.
Completed Cost - Bridge
& approaches: £9,900,000.
Length of Bridge and
approaches: 2 miles 33 chns.
Length of arch span:
1650 FT.
Highest point of arch
above high water: 440 FT.
Height of pylons: 285 FT.
Clearance at high water
for shipping: 170 FT.
Width of arch deck: 160 FT.
Deck Accommodation:
Central roadway 57 FT wide
4 electric railway tracks
(4' 8½" gauge)
2 footways each 10 FT wide.
Bridge commenced
28th July 1923.
Bridge completed
1932.
Bridge opened
19th March
1932.

This message has been received subject to
the Post and Telegraph Act and Regulations

OFFICE OF RECEIPT
OFFICE 23 MAR 1934 EASTWOOD N.S.W.

SYDNEY
Station from HARBOUR BRIDGE Words 50 Time lodged 9 AM No.

C. SCOBELL,
STOREKEEPER RAILWAY PARADE,
EASTWOOD.

GREETINGS   THIS IS ONE OF FIRST TELEGRAMS SENT FROM NEW POSTOFFICE
SITUATED IN SOUTH EASTERN PYLON SYDNEY HARBOUR BRIDGE WHERE WE HAVE
45 PERMANENT EMPLOYEES AND 60 ENTERTAINING ATTRACTIONS IN MOST
AMAZING EXHIBITION IN SOUTHERN HEMISPHERE   URGE YOU VISIT AND SEE
FOR YOURSELF

ARCHER WHITFORD   POSTMASTER
9.15 AM   BC

< George Finey's caricature of Lang, in the midst of the Great Depression, caught both his striking facial appearance and his penchant for aggressive oratory. *Art in Australia*, June 1931.

^ The opening saw a frenzy of souvenir production, with telegrams, train and tram tickets much prized. Spearritt collection, Museum of Sydney

Bridge in the background, the text read: 'AUSTRALIA IS CALLING – Sunshine, Happiness, Opportunity – SYDNEY BRIDGE CELEBRATIONS – March 1932'.

The committee entertained all manner of suggestions about the opening. The Minister for Public Health wanted any royalties on films and souvenirs of the Bridge opening to be paid to the New South Wales Hospitals Commission. The RSL wanted the Bridge to

There were many openings before the final public opening. This is the first party of cars to cross the Bridge on 12 September 1931, though the deck is still strewn with materials and the rail and tram lines are yet to be completed. Dr Bradfield can be seen in typical pose on the far right of the photograph, along with other engineers from Public Works and Dorman Long. Some wives are in attendance. State Records New South Wales NRS12685

The Government of New South Wales requests the honour of the presence of The Honourable W. Brooks, M.L.C. and Mrs. Brooks at the Ceremonies associated with the Official Opening of the Sydney Harbour Bridge by the Honourable J. T. Lang M.L.A. Premier and Colonial Treasurer on Saturday 19th March 1932. His Excellency the Governor Sir Philip W. Game G.B.E. K.C.B. D.S.O. will preside.

Please reply to the Under Secretary, Premier's Department.

On receipt of acceptance card of entrée will be forwarded.

be named ANZAC with a rising sun to be erected on its highest point and each pylon to be called after an arm of the service. Emerson Curtis, one of a number of artists and photographers who produced books about the Bridge, was refused permission to sell his book at the opening. Clearly the committee did not want their event to appear like the showbag pavilion at the Royal Easter Show, so they also rejected a proposal for an Eiffel Tower and ferris wheel. On the other hand they did not want the event to be too sombre, so they quickly quashed a suggestion that the next of kin of the workmen who lost their lives in the construction should be the first to cross the Bridge on the grounds that it would introduce 'an altogether inharmonious note into an official ceremony'.

In January 1932 the committee appealed to all businessmen for assistance because the celebrations would provide 'a stimulus to trade and business through the huge crowds that would be attracted to the city, to create employment, and to advertise the State'.

With the approach of the opening day the committee got down to the nitty-gritty of ceremonial. As the occasion was to be purely 'a State one' they decided that neither the Governor-General nor the Prime Minister need take an 'active part' in the ceremony, though they would of course be invited to watch. Flooded with requests for official seats at the opening, the committee played favourites. Each government minister was allowed 12 tickets to dispense, each MLA four, while Lang and Bradfield got 20 each. Next came the Prime Minister, city aldermen, news proprietors, judges, heads of churches and university representatives, along with Ennis, Freeman and other leading lights in Dorman Long. Only a few of these could fit on the dais or in the Special Reserve section, while the rest were to be seated in miniature grandstands. Benjamin Howe, a former fitter and Labor MLA for North Sydney, was allowed to bring 12 guests and his daughter, while Daniel Clyne, his Labor equivalent on the other side of the harbour, was also allowed 12 guests. The committee was so preoccupied with the matter of seating that they continued to eliminate people to within four days of the event.

> Some of the many floats for the pageant, with soldiers from the Great War in the foreground. *The Bridge Opened*, 1932

v This glass cake dish, with the Harbour Bridge as a serving handle, was one of the most common souvenirs at the time, now a prized collectors' item. Spearritt collection

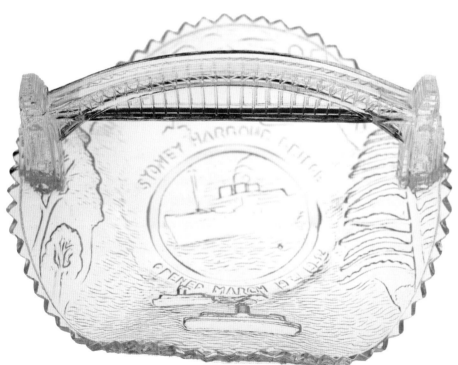

A city of deserted suburbs

And what an event. On 23 March 1932 the *Australian Worker* told its readers that the opening of the Sydney Harbour Bridge brought together 'the largest gathering of people ever seen in Sydney'. Some journalists claimed that 'over a million people' in trains, trams, vehicles and on foot crossed the Bridge during the first 24 hours after it had been opened. The same claim was reprinted in the weekly edition of *The Times* in London. The local, interstate and international press took the figure of 1 million seriously. Such a large gathering of people had never been seen in Sydney, and has only been overtaken once since, on Australia Day 1988, the symbolic highpoint of the Bicentennial celebrations. One reporter, in an attempt to capture the mood of the opening day, chartered a light plane only to find 'a city of deserted suburbs'.

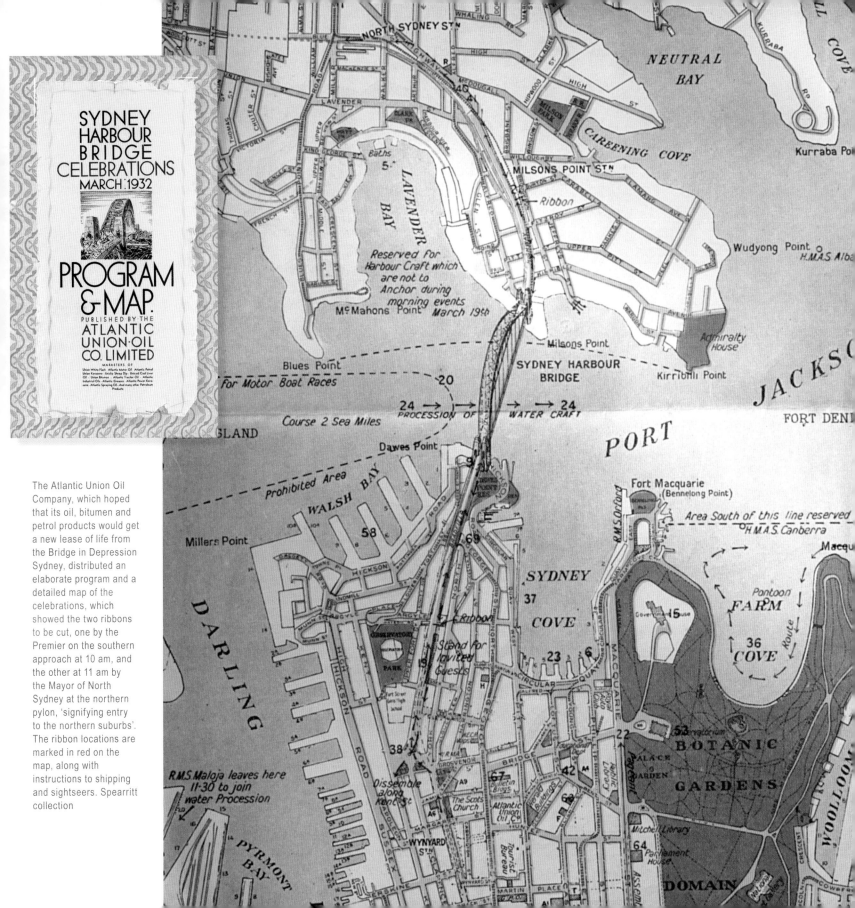

SYDNEY
HARBOUR
BRIDGE
CELEBRATIONS
MARCH 1932

PROGRAM
& MAP.
PUBLISHED BY THE
ATLANTIC
UNION · OIL
CO. LIMITED

MARKETERS OF
Union White Flash · Atlantic Motor Oil · Atlantic Petrol
Union Kerosene · Unidip Sheep Dip · Unicod Cod Liver
Oil · Union Bitumen · Atlantic Tractor Oil · Atlantic
Industrial Oils · Atlantic Greases · Atlantic Power Kero-
sene. Atlantic Spraying Oil. And many other Petroleum
Products

The Atlantic Union Oil Company, which hoped that its oil, bitumen and petrol products would get a new lease of life from the Bridge in Depression Sydney, distributed an elaborate program and a detailed map of the celebrations, which showed the two ribbons to be cut, one by the Premier on the southern approach at 10 am, and the other at 11 am by the Mayor of North Sydney at the northern pylon, 'signifying entry to the northern suburbs'. The ribbon locations are marked in red on the map, along with instructions to shipping and sightseers. Spearritt collection

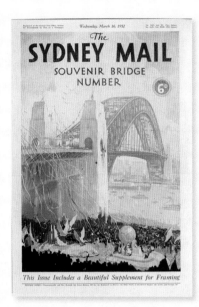

They are the streets as of a city of the dead. No pedestrian, no motorist is seen. Streets, and house, and backyards – devoid of life … below to the left the lifelessness ceases. Hyde Park and the streets that run towards it are choked with people … suddenly one realises that to the west is the focus of all this activity – the bridge, curved like a bow half-drawn … a colossus in its mighty stride [SMH, 21 March 1932].

Reverence for technological progress permeated the entire press coverage of the opening. The celebrations committee tried to mobilise not only their own business acquaintances but the city's children as well. They argued that the opening would leave 'a deep impression on the minds of children to be remembered for years to come, more particularly as they will play an important part in the Pageantry and Church Thanksgiving Services'. The Education Department readily complied, setting aside Wednesday 16 March as Children's Day. Almost 100 000 school pupils crossed the Bridge between 10 am and 3 pm. Although Children's Day was not, according to the Department, to be considered 'in any sense of the word a school holiday', the following Friday was so designated. The churches were not amused, because this congregation of holidays was but a week before Easter. Bishop Crotty of Bathurst wanted a boycott of the Bridge celebrations because the organisers showed scant concern for the 'sacred season' of Lent.

Schoolchildren played a leading part on the great day itself. The band of the Young Australia League was at the head of the opening march, closely followed by 328 schoolchildren and their teachers, the Hurstville Boys Band and a pipe band. Only then came 100 workmen who had taken part in the building of the Bridge, while a party of 20 Aborigines 'specially selected and instructed for the occasion' was led by young Lennie Gwyther who had ridden his pony 965 kilometres from Gippsland in Victoria for the opening. The Aborigines entertained the spectators with popular airs played on gum leaves, on a typical Sydney autumn morning of blue skies and sunshine.

Most sections of society were represented in the pageant one way or another, but unions were not allowed to commemorate their dead comrades. University of Sydney professors of architecture and engineering had a float, while the municipalities of Marrickville, Bankstown and Canterbury presented Captain Cook's ship *Endeavour*. Selected Aborigines played 'popular airs' on gum leaves and finally the public got to 'swarm across', 'a mighty crowd beneath a mighty arch'. *The Bridge Opened*, 1932

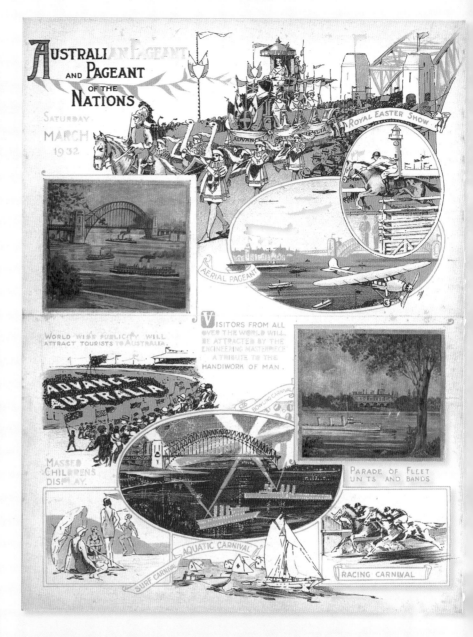

The authorities did everything in their power to concentrate attention on the Bridge itself. Decorations of the Bridge on commercial or government buildings were not permitted. Commented one journalist: 'It was a wise decision, for the admiring thousands saw the structure in all its natural grandeur and beauty.' This decision was in stark contrast to the use of the Bridge in the popular press. Every commercial organisation that could possibly claim any relation to the Bridge (and many that could not) tried to use it as a symbol in their advertising in the special Bridge Opening Supplements produced by all the major papers. A Berlei Foundation Garment advertisement linked the Bridge span to the female form.

Of abiding strength, enduring beauty, a bridge now spans the world's most lovely harbour, draws thousands closer to the city's heart. Berlei corsetry, being actually true to type, provides the one form-fitting foundation which ensures enduring figure beauty for Australian women.

None of this cheap commercialism could detract from the great day itself.

<^ The Berlei foundation garment advertisement from the Official Souvenir and Programme, published by the New South Wales Government Printer. The back cover of the four page fundraising brochure promised an elaborate pageant. Spearritt collection

How de Groot beat Lang to the ribbon

vThis cartoon appeared in *Smith's Weekly* on 17 March 1932, two days before the official opening. This may have given de Groot the idea to get to the ribbon first.

A meticulous recent biography of Irish-born Francis de Groot by Andrew Moore, has shown how Eric Campbell, the leader of the New Guard, and Francis de Groot, one of his four zone commanders, successfully executed a symbolic blow against Lang at the opening of the Bridge. Campbell even told a public meeting at Lane Cove that 'Mr Lang will not open the Bridge.' Two days before the opening de Groot saw in *Smith's Weekly* a Joe Johnson cartoon 'the man who beat Lang to the tape' and hatched his plan, with Campbell's knowledge and co-operation. Like other leading New Guardsmen, both men were under close scrutiny by the New South Wales Police and Commonwealth Investigation Branch agents, who had infiltrated the group's main decision-making body, fearful of an outbreak of violence from the paramilitary organisation, sworn opponents of Lang and 'communists'.

Forecast of the Unrehearsed Bridge Incident

THE MAN WHO BEAT LANG TO THE TAPE

OFFICIAL PICTURE OF THE OPENING CEREMONY

∧ Sydney University students produced an 'unofficial souvenir' of the opening ceremony, including a procession with 'Kernel Uric Dumbell, Bleeder of the New Guard' and full page cartoons of Bradfield and Freeman both claiming 'Alone I Did It'. The front cover of the brochure has Lang telling Governor Game to 'Hop it' and the Dorman Long engineer Freeman telling Bradfield 'It's My Design, I Tell Yer'. Spearritt collection

Colonel Campbell remained at home on the day of the opening to put the police off the scent. A couple of days before the opening de Groot actually told his surveiling officers that he would open the Bridge on horseback, disguised as Ned Kelly. The two detectives who heard this, and knew de Groot better than most, were lulled into a false sense of security by the implausible plot, and instead of attending the opening ceremony they went to a pub in Market Street.

De Groot borrowed a girl's horse from a paddock in Turramurra, arranged to have it shod, while accomplices transported it the following morning on the horse punt from Milsons Point to Dawes Point. Attired in Campbell's ex-AIF tunic and gear from his time in the Hussars, de Groot managed to join a troop of the Royal New South Wales Lancers leaving Government House near Macquarie Street as they moved through the city at a brisk trot. As they approached the official dais de Groot survived the scrutiny of the Governor-General and the nearby mounted police. Hiding behind Ken Hall's high-sided Cinesound van he remain undetected. Lang had 100 yards to walk to the 70 feet of blue silk ribbon. Pretending that he was having difficulty in controlling his horse, de Groot – who did not want to appear to be attacking the Premier, as he might be shot on the spot – finally managed to get to the ribbon but couldn't cut it on his first try and had to lift it with his left hand to cut it with his sword. He then declared, into the nearby microphone, the Bridge open 'on behalf of the decent and respectable citizens of New South Wales'.

De Groot's ride meant different things to

different people. The *Sydney Mail* dismissed it as a 'slight contretemps' which added to the excitement of the proceedings. To one *Herald* letter writer it was a reminder to the world 'that there is a very large section of New South Wales which dislikes repudiation, class legislation, political vindictiveness and all the other detestable things which Langism stands for'. To the cameramen of the press it meant personal and professional embarrassment. As Ken Hall, the manager of Cinesound Newsreel tells it,

> The newspapermen were fifty yards away up in their elevated box. I've never seen anything quite as funny as those Press boys falling, scrambling, jumping out of that box, dropping their cameras, yelling abuse, swearing dreadfully, but getting there too late. We had the only pictures and the newspapers and wire services came smartly knocking on our door. We made many duplicates and gave them out for free. The pictures hit the front pages of course. (*Autobiography*, 1977)

For many people who attended the opening the newsreel picture was the first they knew of the incident. Ab Harris who turned 17 in 1932, left his Burwood home at 8.30 on the Saturday morning and travelled by train direct to Wynyard. He had no difficulty in finding a possie for the procession on the stone fence in front of Fort Street Girls High School. He did not realise that de Groot had cut the ribbon until he was on his way home and picked up an early afternoon edition of the *Sun*. Cinesound Newsreel deserved its world scoop. Hall knew that the New Guard had claimed that Lang would never open the Bridge and continued to take their threat seriously, placing cameramen at strategic points for the 'great day', 'including Lang's home in the Sydney suburb of Auburn, where I thought they might try to bottle him up'.

With the official opening over, the Historical Pageant could begin. Floats came from everywhere. On one, a latter-day Captain Cook stood in front of a model of the *Endeavour* accompanied by 'two dusky aborigines in full war paint'. On the Eastern Suburbs float bronzed male lifesavers were accompanied by 'a bevy of local girls attired as mermaids'. The spectacle of lovely girls on the 'mighty Sydney Harbour Bridge' captured the attention of many a male journalist. Some floats had their amusing side. Someone forgot to include sandshoes for the Bondi lifesaver's float, and by midday when the procession was in full flight the bronzed lifesavers appeared to be dancing. In fact their feet were blistering on the hot asphalt roadway.

Pedestrian traffic began on the footways and roadways of the Bridge after the pageant had dispersed. As the Hobart *Mercury* put it, 'so the great roadway will be open to the people', who swarmed upon it. Pedestrians had the freedom of the roadway until midnight when vehicular traffic started. Earlier in the afternoon the railway and tramway tracks across the Bridge were brought into service, linking the northern suburbs with the city for the first time. Although the harbour figured largely in the day's proceedings, in the evening it really came into its own.

> At times the moving searchlights paused in their play and concentrated their beams on the great arch of the bridge ... and with that vision of etherealised steel lingering in their memories the thronging thousands 'turned again home', tired, satisfied, and happy [*Sydney Mail*, 23 March 1932].

COLONEL CAMPBELL — MISTER LANG

Composed by
JOHN QUINLAN

Regal Record
No. G.21551

Published by
Jack O'Hagan Music Pty. Ltd.
239 Collins Street, Melbourne, C.1
'Phone: Cent. 8461

POPULAR EDITION 6D. NET

< Sheet music for a satirical song published in 1932. Spearritt collection

> During the Great Depression there was widespread concern about how the New South Wales government could pay back the London and New York financiers who had lent the money for the Bridge. At one point Lang's Labor government contemplated selling a lease on the Bridge for a two year period to raise some money. The Bridge has always remained in State government ownership. *Smith's Weekly*, 26 March 1932

> Even Lifesavers,
the sweet manufacturers,
produced a commemorative
booklet titled simply
Achievement, 1932

v Salt and pepper
shakers with an image
from North Sydney, c 1936.
Spearritt collection

THE MORNING AFTER: Dummy takes up his burden.

The shadow behind the Bridge

Hailed by both the Labor and the capitalist
newspapers as the achievement of the century, the
Bridge also featured in every imaginable magazine.
Newspapers such as the *Sydney Morning Herald*, the *Sun*
and the *Telegraph* produced large supplements in its
honour. Articles about all aspects of the construction
were accompanied by pages of advertisements
as businesses vied with each other to bask in the
Bridge's reflected glory. Typical of the reaction of
employers to the Bridge was the advertisement placed
by the men's and boys' outfitters, FJ Palmer's, on the
front page of the *Labor Daily*:

Today is the day of days, when political differences
are forgotten, New South Wales unites in the

A SOUVENIR WHICH WILL BECOME HISTORICAL

A MAGNIFICENT SOUVENIR
OF THE
SYDNEY BRIDGE CELEBRATIONS

To be ready March 1st

Published by
ART IN AUSTRALIA LTD.

THIS handsome souvenir of the Sydney Bridge Celebrations will be beautifully printed on the finest paper, and will be published for sale early in March. The book will contain articles and illustrations, many of which will be in colour.

THE designs for the various pageants to be held on March 19th (the opening day of the Bridge) will be printed in colour—and they will all be accurately described.

A MAGNIFICENT series of full page photographic studies of Sydney by the world-famous photographer E. O. Hoppe will be included, and a fine series of photographs by H. Cazneaux on the Bridge—with other studies will form part of the book. Articles on Sydney—on the Bridge—the Royal Show—on sporting activities including surfing will be in the book.

It will be a comprehensive book on Sydney, perhaps the finest record yet compiled. The historical side will be dealt with and also the commercial life of the city. Studies of the underground railway and an excellent series of paintings of Sydney by prominent artists.

For the modest price of 3/6 the public will be offered a handsome volume which will be as good as anything yet attempted by an Australian publishing firm. Every effort is being made to make this an outstanding and worthy publication, suitable for such an occasion.

Advertising space is being rapidly booked—intending advertisers are asked to write — Advertising Manager, Art in Australia Ltd.—for rates, etc. Size of book 12½ x 9½ ins.

< Postage stamps, commemorative certificates, special issues of magazines and newspapers all celebrated the triumph of the Bridge opening. The most elegant production was *Art in Australia*'s Sydney Bridge Celebrations (advertisement from *Home* magazine January 1932)

glorification of the Our Bridge, an added attraction to Our Harbour. The building of this gigantic bridge is just as much a national milestone as Anzac [19 March 1932].

During the 1930s the Bridge became a symbol for the city, a prosperous symbol, planned in better times. In the middle of the Depression it was a sign that a return to the prosperous city was possible. It was a symbol worth capturing and Lang was pleased that a Labor Premier would open it. Had a non-Labor government been in power it might well have invited royalty to the occasion. The Duke and Duchess of York had opened the new Parliament House in Canberra in 1927. In 1934 the Duke of Gloucester officiated at the opening of the Victorian government's Centenary celebrations.

The only sour notes about the opening were sounded in the left-wing press. The Australian Workers Union newspaper, *Australian Worker*, carried a dramatic cartoon, 'The Shadow Behind the Bridge'. But the cartoon was critical of the Depression, not of the Bridge itself, which had given work to thousands. A similar attitude was taken by the Communist *Workers' Weekly*. It too shared in the bipartisan praise for the Bridge, and the scientific and technical accomplishment it represented. However, its coverage was more specifically ideological:

> The bridge is certainly a fine example of science, of technique, a lesson of what human labour can accomplish. Despite all the technical skills and science which the bridge typifies, the Capitalist system cannot find work and proper food and housing for its wage slaves. There is the huge bridge, and on the opposite side of the street, the slums created by Capitalism … The capitalists cry out about the achievement of the bridge, but when we compare it with what is being achieved under Socialism in the USSR, we at once comprehend the startling contrasts [25 March 1932].

In the first months after the Bridge's completion its shadow lengthened as unemployment worsened and Lang's government tottered on the brink of financial and constitutional crisis. On 13 May, Lang was dismissed by the State Governor, Sir Philip Game, who called a general election. Lang accepted

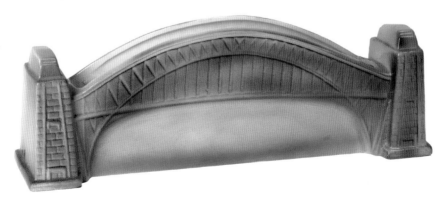

< Ceramic vase in the shape of the Bridge and Bridge crossing certificate. Spearritt collection, Museum of Sydney

89

^ > The range of souvenir items varied from professional products to amateur productions. The biscuit tin dates from the time of the opening. The hair brush and comb date from the 1950s. Spearritt collection, Museum of Sydney

his dismissal although its legality has been debated ever since. On 19 May, nearly 400 Bridge workers were laid off. A general election was set for 11 June and the threat of unemployment was used by major firms in an attempt to sway the working-class vote. The number of seats held by Labor in both metropolitan and country areas was more than halved. Labor dropped from the 55 seats it had won in the 1930 landslide to 24, and managed to retain only 14 of its 29 Sydney seats. Lang's attempt to identify himself with the Bridge – later satirised by cartoonists as 'Lang's Coathanger' – did not do him any good on the North Shore, where Labor lost its only stronghold, North Sydney.

Although opened in the worst year of the Depression, few thought of the Bridge then or since as anything other than a symbol in which every social class could share. The construction, opening and self-satisfied contemplation of the completed Bridge embodied a consensus which goes a long way to explain the lack of radical class-consciousness among the bulk of the working class in Depression Sydney.

In a society without mass rituals the opening of the Sydney Harbour Bridge proved an unusual event. It provided the populace with a chance to participate in a most dramatic way, by walking over or in fact through it. Few other structures or events provide such an opportunity. Contrast the Bridge opening with the passive role played by the crowds

90

KNOWLEDGE · EXPERIENCE · ORGANISATION

The World

ALL the knowledge and experience gained over thirty years of organising have gone to the publication of "*The World*," Sydney's great afternoon daily newspaper.

A democratic paper, intensely Australian in its outlook, "*The World*" is produced by one of the finest Newspaper Staffs ever assembled in Australia.

The immediate popularity of "*The World*" and its ever-increasing circulation indicate how accurately the needs of the Sydney public have been gauged.

Reliable, dignified, powerful, "*The World*" already penetrates into the homes of at least one-third of Sydney's metropolitan population.

A great newspaper
and a great advertising medium.

– even for the few thousand who got near the dais – when Queen Elizabeth II opened the Sydney Opera House in 1973. Unlike that event the Bridge opening took place before television. Certainly many people, notably in the New South Wales countryside and in other States, listened to the radio (40 stations engaged in simultaneous broadcasts) and people around the world saw at least a still from the Cinesound Newsreel of de Groot beating Lang to the ribbon. But to experience the great day you had to be there, which is one reason why such a large proportion of Sydney's population actually turned up. The Bridge and its immediate surrounds were large enough to hold them all.

∨ The cast iron map of Australia, with an electric radiator coil (missing) and a detachable Harbour Bridge grill was made in a local foundry and sold door to door in Sydney during the depression. Spearritt collection, Museum of Sydney

< The advertisement from *The World*, a left-wing newspaper which stressed the majesty of the construction process and the final edifice, appeared in the *Sydney Harbour Bridge Official Souvenir Programme*

Blood on the pylons

When the Bridge opened on 19 March 1932 the Australian Workers Union (AWU) paper The World, founded just five months before, hailed it as enthusiastically as the anti-Labor press.

Their headline 'MIGHTY SYMBOL OF A CENTURY'S PROGRESS' made their approval clear. But there was a solemn note in their coverage. Their young assistant editor, Brian Fitzpatrick, who had worked on both the Melbourne *Age* and the Sydney *Daily Telegraph*, published his poem 'Bridge Builders'. The fifth stanza read:

There's blood upon the pylons; see
Pathetic on the stone
A tablet for the eight men we
Remember died alone.

As *The World* reminded its readers, more than eight men had died both on and off the structure in the seven years of preparation and building. In a 'Lest We Forget' column, surrounded by a black border, *The World* listed eight ironworkers, one painter, one AWU member and two quarrymen, telling its readers:

These men gave their lives that we might cross the mighty structure which spans the Harbour. These are the soldiers of industry who are counted in the cost of the Bridge. It is customary, in the rejoicing over

< Emerson Curtis, a young artist, captured the drama and the danger of construction on both the Bridge and in the Dorman Long workshops in his line drawings, published in 1933 in an elegant folio *Building the Bridge*

a victory, to give a thought to those who have lain down their lives to procure it. Let us, therefore, give a thought today to these brave warriors who fought, with their comrades, to conquer the forces of nature with their steel plates and girders, that you and I might save ten minutes in our daily rush to and from the city.

The metaphor of war appears often in writing about the building of the Bridge; to explain – though not to justify – the deaths. In *The World's* account the Bridge became an altar to progress at which lives of workers were sacrificed.

One dogman lifts Moruya granite on a crane while another lifts steel reinforcing. Both are working to complete the top sections of the pylons. The danger is obvious. State Records New South Wales NRS12685, December 1931

"One Day I Fell Off Sydney Harbor Bridge..."

ONLY one man has ever been able to say that.

He is VINCENT ROY KELLY, who, on October 23, 1930, was riveting on the decking of the Harbor Bridge, Sydney, then being built. He slipped and fell 175 feet to the water. Kelly struck the water feet first. Uppers of his boots were torn from the soles and forced up his legs. He was injured internally. Taken to hospital he was unconscious two weeks.

—175 FT

The Drop which Riveter Kelly survived was taken as a way of death by such a number of suicides, after the bridge was finished, authorities had to erect present barbed-wire guards on railings.

The Sydney press liked to play up the dangers and press photographers loved the Bridge as a dramatic subject. The photograph of the deck hanging is from the time that Kelly fell, in October 1930, while the later photo of him on the facing page was *Smith's Weekly*'s way of completing the story

Soldiers of industry

The first deaths caused by the construction of the Bridge happened in 1926. On 7 April 1926, Harry Waters, a 50-year-old dogman, was injured at the Moruya quarry and died the next day. A few months later Robert Craig, a 63-year-old braceman and member of the Ironworkers Union, died after falling from the approach spans onto the Millers Point ballast heap. Contemporary film of both the Moruya quarry and the Bridge construction shows just how dangerous conditions were. Although the quarry was only 100 metres from the wharf, moving the blocks even that distance posed difficulties. The most dangerous activity was blasting, which on one occasion produced a block of granite weighing 200 tonnes, with dimensions of 16.8 by 7.6 by 5.5 metres. In March 1927 the quarry claimed another life, 30-year-old Percival Poole.

Working on the Bridge was inherently dangerous not only because of its great height but because of the construction techniques used. To take one example among many: most

^ A busy scene in the Dorman Long workshops in April 1930, where steel joists are being assembled. While not as dangerous as working on the Bridge itself, there were many injuries and some deaths in the workshops. State Records New South Wales NRS12685

of the 6 million rivets in the structure were individually heated *in situ* by workmen and then handed over – in a semi-molten state – to be hammered in. Though the workmen wore goggles the risks were still grave. Many rivets were inserted on the structure itself, while others were used in the workshops for fabrication purposes. With a total weight of 3200 tonnes, 100 000 rivets were judged faulty by inspectors and had to be cut out and replaced. The *Sydney Morning Herald* offered a romantic view of the process:

> The rivetters, tossing incandescent pieces of steel to each other, like playful satans, pin the plates and the angles together, and to other plates and angles and you find the dirty, twisted metal of the wharf transformed into a complex mass of stanchions, stiffeners, and cross beams, which are as certain to fit other units as the sun is to rise over the east of Sydney tomorrow [21 January 1928].

Five weeks later, William Woods of Five Dock fell 21 metres from a gantry at Milsons Point to his death. Just three months earlier, on 6 December 1927, Nathaniel Swandells, a 22-year-old riveter from Scotland, fell from the eighth span and drowned.

Two deaths in the space of three months was not, as the unions saw it, a good record. On 6 April 1928 engineers working on the Bridge were awarded a height allowance because of the 'exacting nature' of the work. There were no more deaths in 1928 but disputes over pay and working conditions were many. On 17 April crane drivers stopped work for the day over increased pay demands.

The Employers Federation complained about increases granted to Bridge employees in early June 1928, and especially the fact that many of their applications were supported by Dorman Long (who lost nothing, because as specified in the

contract, all wage increases were to be paid by the government) and Bradfield. The Federation 'while realising that it was highly desirable to complete this important undertaking within the specified time, was of the opinion that the government should more closely watch the position of these increases, and safeguard the interests of the taxpayers'. Over the whole period of construction the extra wages bill for the New South Wales government amounted to almost £800 000. It appears that Dorman Long preferred to support most wage rises, because these cost them nothing, whereas a dramatic improvement in working conditions and safety precautions would have cost them plenty.

Boilermakers walked off the job in early September 1928 claiming that the work was too 'dangerous' and demanding higher pay for working at 'extreme height'. They were soon joined by 120 ironworkers. Both groups demanded 'double-pay' so that shifts could be halved without loss of pay to the men. They argued that in a shift of 4 hours and 24 minutes there would be less chance of a man 'losing his nerve' than in a full-length shift. The press regularly reported the repeated demands of engineers, riggers, boilermakers and ironworkers for increased rates of pay and shorter hours. The Melbourne *Argus* interviewed James Winning, a riveter, who said that

> under existing conditions work on the Harbour Bridge was unnatural for any human being. It was different from anything he had ever experienced. He thought that the working day should be reduced to 4 hours. Frequently, when putting in rivets, he had only his feet to hang on with, at an angle of 45 degrees [23 March 1929].

On 26 March Thomas McKeon, 48-year-old rigger, was working with three others on a platform 50 metres up, when the platform slipped. Two of the

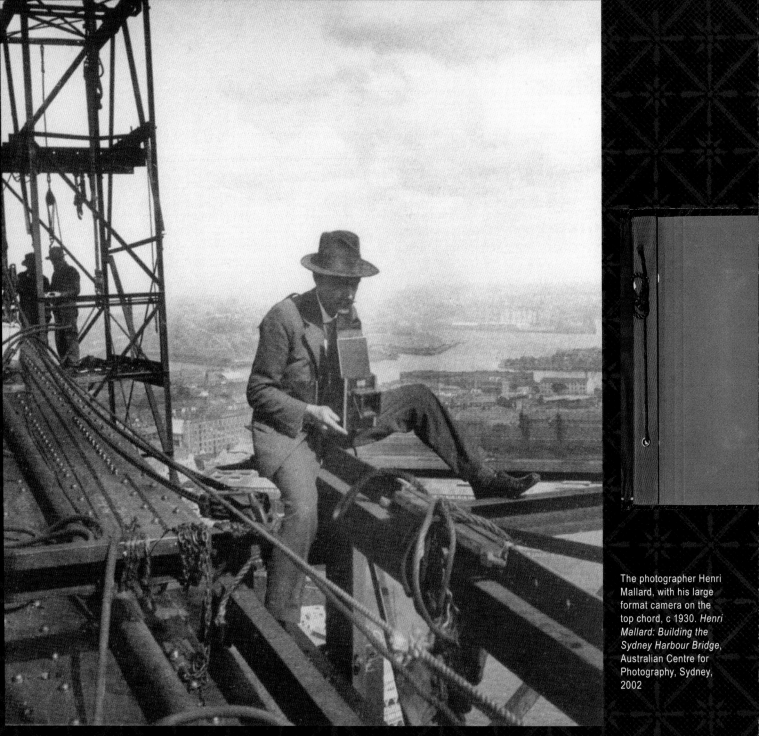

The photographer Henri
Mallard, with his large
format camera on the
top chord, c 1930. *Henri
Mallard: Building the
Sydney Harbour Bridge*,
Australian Centre for
Photography, Sydney,
2002

men managed to hold on to the fixtures and get to safety but McKeon, as the *Argus* graphically reported it,

> fell away from all supports, and the only object which he could grasp was a chain on one of the cranes. The chain, however, was descending and he became entangled in it. One of his legs and one hand were torn off when he fell to the ground. He was dead when his workmates reached him.

By the time of McKeon's death, three men had died on the Bridge itself, two in the Bridge workshops and two in the Moruya quarries. The latter four were overlooked by the press because they were not as spectacular as the Bridge deaths. McKeon's death was headlined as the 'third bridge fatality'.

A day after McKeon's death Judge Beeby announced substantial wage increases for Bridge workers, saying:

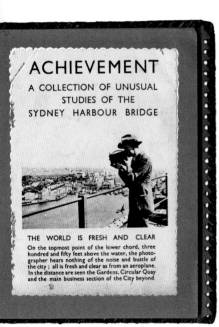

ACHIEVEMENT

A COLLECTION OF UNUSUAL STUDIES OF THE SYDNEY HARBOUR BRIDGE

THE WORLD IS FRESH AND CLEAR

On the topmost point of the lower chord, three hundred and fifty feet above the water, the photographer hears nothing of the noise and bustle of the city ; all is fresh and clear as from an aeroplane. In the distance are seen the Gardens, Circular Quay and the main business section of the City beyond.

> A community which asks such unusual service must be prepared to offer unusual wages … For the next 18 months from 100 to 150 workers will be engaged from day to day on a venture which is exciting the interest of the engineering world. The men are engaged in one of the world's most difficult and hazardous engineering undertakings [*Argus*, 28 March 1929].

For work on the first seven panels from each pylon pay rates were to be 60 per cent greater and for the 14 centre panels 75 per cent greater. The pay increases were made retrospective to 22 January, scant consolation for Thomas McKeon. Most of the Bridge dead were unmarried and without dependants. They received burial expenses but no compensation for their relatives.

The next fatality occurred almost a year to the day of McKeon's death. On 6 March 1930

25-year-old Sidney Addison of Naremburn fell 50 metres from the partly constructed arch. He had been tightening a nut in the steel fabric of the northern side when the spanner slipped and he fell backwards. He struck the water and drowned before his companions could reach him. The hundreds of men then working on the Bridge ceased work – no doubt with the thought that they might suffer the same fate – until the 'shock of the fatality had passed'. Some men working at dangerous altitudes went home for the day.

The shock of Addison's death was such that the men took what extra care they could and there were no more fatalities in 1930. But in March 1931 John Faulkner, a 40-year-old rigger, was struck by a huge iron plate and died shortly afterwards. In July James Chilvers, a 52-year-old dogman, was knocked from the workshop wharf into the harbour and drowned. Later in the same month John Henry Webb, a 23-year-old painter, fell to his death from the Bridge. The more spectacular the death, the more likely the press was to publish a full account. Just five weeks before the opening, the *Labor Daily* (then controlled by Langites) published a graphic account of the death of James Campbell, a 45-year-old foreman rigger of Milsons Point.

> Campbell had been engaged in dismantling the scaffolding near the top of the pylon. A strong gust of wind moved the beam on which he was standing, and he was hurtled into space. Horrified watchers in the streets below saw him shot out from the pylon, turning over and over as he clutched wildly for something to stay his flight … He fell through the open structure near the footway to the ground, 150 feet below [10 February 1932].

Although the *Labor Daily* headlined the event 'Man's Grim Death in Fall from Pylon', Campbell's death was treated as inevitable, with no accompanying criticism about the almost non-existent safety precautions on the Bridge. Likewise the AWU's paper the *Australian Worker* carried a brief account of their 'comrade's death', but again no comment about the lack of safety precautions.

Sixteen men died in the construction of the Bridge and related work in the fabrication shops and at the Moruya quarry. Compared with many other large construction jobs – and it was one of the largest in Australia's history, taking seven years – it was not a high toll, though a number of men had miraculous escapes. Nor is it a high toll when compared to that on some other bridges in Australia, especially those where major accidents occurred. The collapse of one span during the construction of the Westgate Bridge in Melbourne in October 1970 claimed 35 lives. And it is easy to forget that the construction of virtually every high-rise block in Australia – whether offices or flats – claims at least one life. One quarter of all construction deaths in Australia are height related. Industrial accidents are rarely given prominence in the press unless they are spectacular, and they are soon forgotten, except of course by the union, work companions and relatives of the victims. While the death toll on the Bridge is comparable to similar projects, it could have been lower. Safety regulations scarcely existed and it is amazing that there were not more deaths. Dorman Long could have erected safety nets, like those under the Golden Gate Bridge (opened in 1937) that saved 19 men on that site. Many men lost limbs or fingers, a virtually unavoidable consequence of the hot rivet construction methods, but their injuries were so frequent that the press did not bother to report them. Even the left-wing and union press made relatively little of the deaths and injuries, which were usually depicted as an unfortunate but inevitable consequence of high-risk jobs and the price of 'progress'.

The day after James Campbell died a Roseville reader wrote to the *Herald*:

> Many of your readers, especially those from the North Shore, who have watched the bridge growing to completion, must have been greatly shocked in reading of the tragic death of the foreman rigger. After all, despite the 'machine age' in which we live, such structures as the bridge would never get beyond the stage of being merely pretty pictures on the draughtsman's board if it were not for the daring and resource of such men, who hourly take their lives in their hands … At this late hour, might I suggest that 'the men who actually did the job' have some line of recognition on the tablet, setting forth the parts played by the several parties on this monument of engineering skill and workmanship [10 February 1932].

The Official Organising Committee for the Bridge opening, which included Premier Jack Lang, did not take up the suggestion. The Bridge workers got praise instead. A couple of days before the opening Lawrence Ennis, director of construction for Dorman Long told members of the 'Smith Family, Joyspreaders Unlimited' that the work had been difficult and dangerous. He went on to say, in an uncharacteristic comment against the class he represented, that there had been

> much talk from people who knew all about bridge building – from armchairs and verandahs round the harbour (laughter) about the wages they paid to the men. I can tell you now, that the men, with the exception of one or two, have not received one penny more than they were entitled to. Every day those men went on to the Bridge, they went in the same way as a soldier goes into battle, not knowing whether they would come down alive or not [SMH, 17 March 1932].

Again, the metaphor of war. It was perhaps an easy point for the Dorman Long big wig to make, as his

∧ The author chatting to a painter on the top chord, 1981. Photograph by John Storey

company did not have to foot the bill for higher wages, but it did at least put the workers' case to the bourgeoisie – who rarely risked their lives in their jobs.

In April 1932 the remaining workers, most of whom were now employees of the Public Works Department (with responsibility for finishing touches on the rail and tram tracks) were gradually dismissed by Lang's Labor government, only to find themselves thrown onto the job market in the worst year of the Depression. Some unions, most notably the carpenters', attempted to organise strike action but were unsuccessful. The Depression

dragging on without respite had sapped union militancy.

All the commemorative plaques were in place by the end of April. Only then did the Darling Harbour branch of the Australian Labor Party finally manage to persuade the Labor government that a tablet to the dead Bridge workers should be installed. In early May the Lord Mayor's commemorative tablet was moved from the western to the eastern parapet wall and a heavy bronze plaque, 120 by 30 centimetres, dedicated to the 16 workmen who lost their lives in the construction of the Bridge, was erected, with little ceremony, in its place.

> The Roads and Traffic Authority have been removing lead paint from the Bridge in an enclosed gantry structure, with much more elaborate health and safety precautions than have ever prevailed before. Photograph by John Storey, Dawes Point, 2006

285ft.

< This Minties advertisement, which appeared in *Smith's Weekly* on the opening day, 19 March 1932, reveals sensible fears about the impact of an accident on the Bridge. Horse-drawn vehicles still used the Bridge in the early years of its opening, while traffic accidents gradually became grimmer, with more traffic and greater speeds

∧ Until the recent voluntary agreement among the media not to report most suicides, this topic used to be a staple for the tabloid press. The *Sun Herald* told its readers on 3 November 1963 that 'a housewife plunged to her death from the Harbour Bridge yesterday after failing to keep a hospital appointment'. The photograph showed the extent of her fall

Driven to death

In the 80 years since the opening the safety record for Bridge workers, including both painters and public transport employees, has been excellent, with only two recorded deaths: CE Webb, killed during the trial maintenance period in early 1932, and Sallie Scheffer, a 62-year-old Bridge painter who fell 30 metres to his death from the Dawes Point catwalk at 7.30 am on 15 March 1979.

But the Bridge soon became the focus of a different kind of death: suicide. For a time it replaced 'The Gap' at Watsons Bay as Sydney's leading locale for suicides; in the seven months after its opening at the height of the Depression 60 people jumped to their deaths. By October the numbers had become so alarming that a North Sydney councillor thought the Bridge was gaining an 'unenviable reputation' and suggested the weapon of ridicule. A springboard could be placed at some convenient spot, with a notice indicating a charge of 1 shilling per head for those who wished to use it. His suggestion was not implemented, but the height of the pedestrian balustrade was raised by wire mesh topped with barbed wire, forcing future would-be suicides to be more resourceful.

With that avenue all but closed off the Pylon Lookout became a popular spot for suicides. It too became inaccessible on its closure in 1971. When re-opened by the Department of Main Roads (DMR) in 1982, its external viewing area had extra security measures to prevent jumping off.

The *Medical Journal of Australia* of 28 May 1983, reports the findings of PM Harvey and BJ Solomons. These two medical researchers examined 89 suicide leaps from the Bridge between 1932 and 1982, 57 of them before the safety fence was erected in 1934. Eighty-five per cent of people who jumped died, and of the handful of survivors, half of them hit the water feet first. The warm and usually calm waters of Port Jackson combined with the proximity of the Sydney Water Police boatshed helped in prompt recovery, especially during daylight hours.

< Suicides from the Pylon Lookout were common until the Department of Main Roads closed it in 1971. In its modern guise the Pylon Lookout has extensive railing and a security guard in attendance. Rescuers managed to persuade this woman to return to safety. *Sun*, 2 March 1971

v Sallie Scheffer, a 62-year-old Bridge painter fell to his death from the Dawes Point approaches while applying undercoat at 7.30 am on 15 March 1979. He is the only Bridge worker to fall to his death since the Bridge was completed. P Spearritt, *The Sydney Harbour Bridge: a life* 1982, p 71

PAINTER FALLS FROM CATWALK

What was the attraction of the Bridge as a suicide site? In an age before drugs became a readily available and publicised form of suicide, any kind of tall structure was attractive to those wishing to kill themselves. Instant death was almost certain, and for those who desired it, posthumous publicity was guaranteed until newspapers, in the 1990s, agreed to curtail their reporting of other than celebrity suicides, not least to discourage copycats.

In recent years most would-be suicides have been attempted from the pedestrian or cycle ways, as Bridge Climb and tight security measures have made the bottom and top chords of the Bridge virtually inaccessible. Intoxicated people can no longer go for a midnight climb. In 2005, to stop people jumping in front of trains from the cycleway on the western side, the Roads and Traffic Authority (RTA) erected wire mesh on top of the balustrade abutting the railway tracks and did the same on the eastern, pedestrian walkway, abutting the roadway. Camera surveillance now alerts security guards of suicidal intentions.

The main cause of death on the Bridge since the 1940s has been road accidents. Because of the demand on the Bridge and the necessity to change lanes for peak hours it has not been possible to erect a barrier between south- and north-bound traffic. The result has been a number of head-on collisions. Many more accidents occur through careless lane changing or in poor weather conditions, especially after light rain. Although the surface of the Bridge roadway is maintained in excellent condition by the RTA, it is impossible to prevent a certain build-up of oil. There would be few people who regularly drive across the Bridge who have not witnessed at least one serious accident. Perhaps even the most secular among us reflect, as did those workmen eight decades before, 'there, but for the grace of God, go I'.

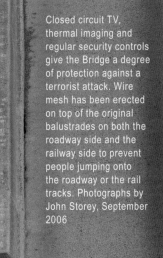

Closed circuit TV, thermal imaging and regular security controls give the Bridge a degree of protection against a terrorist attack. Wire mesh has been erected on top of the original balustrades on both the roadway side and the railway side to prevent people jumping onto the roadway or the rail tracks. Photographs by John Storey, September 2006

∨ 'Even at one a.m. ... The traffic crossing the Bridge piled up quickly early today'. This accident blocked several lanes. For some years lane changing was prohibited. Fairfax Photo Library, 29 May 1972

The terrorist threat

The destruction of the seemingly impregnable twin towers of the World Trade Centre in New York on 11 September 2001 and the bombing of a night club frequented by Australians in Bali in October 2002 made Australia much more conscious of international terrorist threats, especially from Islamic jihadists. The Sydney Olympics, where modest security measures were in place, had been mercifully free of any terror incidents, unlike the Munich Olympics in 1972.

Intriguingly, the Sydney Harbour Bridge didn't rate a mention or a question in the New South Wales Parliament from 1991–2002. But in September 2003, by which time the Bridge, the Opera House and the Anzac Bridge had all been identified by State and Commonwealth police as potential terrorist targets, the Roads and Traffic Authority (successor to the DMR) recommended the addition of thermal imaging cameras to augment the security staff patrolling the structure and the closed circuit TV cameras already in place. With the bombing of the Australian Embassy in Jakarta in September 2004, further measures were announced by Premier Carr in February 2005, including cameras which could not only identify the movement of people but detect whether any out of place objects were present, such as an unattended bag.

To date the measures are not intrusive for train passengers, car drivers or pedestrians. One doesn't have to go through a security screen to cross the Bridge, unlike entering an airport. But any attack on the Bridge could claim thousands of lives and plunge the city's transport system into disarray, as we saw with the bombing attacks on public transport in Madrid in 2004 and London in 2005.

105

Paying and using

Whenever a major new road, bridge
or tunnel is built the question arises as to how it
will be paid for and whether users will have to
pay a toll. Toll roads have existed for well
over 2000 years. Tolls have always been charged
on most vehicular ferries in Australia, both in
the horse-drawn and motor era.

Most railways in Australia were built by government, not by private interests, unlike the United Kingdom and the United States. The colonial and, after federation, State governments borrowed money, usually from the United Kingdom. The taxes they levied paid for interest on the loans while revenue from rail passengers and freight offset the high cost of providing and maintaining the rolling stock, the stations, the tracks and the wages of a huge workforce. Sometimes the New South Wales Railway Commissioners made a profit on freight and passenger services, especially before the rise of the car and the truck. Bradfield conceived his grand city and suburban railway and Harbour Bridge plans at the dawn of the age of the motor vehicle. But well before then vested interests in favour of a Bridge had speculated about how it could be paid for and who should pay for it.

^ *Gregory's Guide to Sydney,*1954 shows the location of surfing beaches to the north and south of the Harbour Bridge. By the time this map was drawn trams were being phased out, and no longer went beyond the Spit Bridge. Trams still serviced the southern beaches, but increasingly leisure trips happened by car.

< Originally conceived by Bradfield as a rail and road bridge, with four sets of rail tracks, the decision to give the two eastern tracks to trams, a measure thought to be temporary at the time, shows that such a seemingly solid structure can be changed. In this 1959 photograph the tramlines have already been removed and toll booths are being built for the two eastern lanes of traffic, which would lead both directly into the city and onto the recently opened Cahill Expressway to the eastern suburbs. Department of Main Roads photograph, 1959

> Both the tram tracks being installed on the eastern side of the Bridge and the railway tracks being installed on the western side entered tunnels visible in the background. The tram tunnels came out near Wynyard while the trains remained underground till they resurfaced beyond Town Hall station. State Records New South Wales NRS12685, 1931

< This banner, from a North Sydney religious group, is likely to have been used on the opening day. Spearritt collection, Museum of Sydney

NORTH SYDNEY
HOME LEAGUE

"BLESSED BE THE TIE THAT BINDS OUR HOMES IN CHRISTIAN LOVE"

Should the North Shore pay?

When the Sydney and North Shore Junction League published its manifesto for a link between the city and North Sydney in 1906, it brushed aside self-interest in an elegant disclaimer:

> The proposal put forward by the league to connect the City of Sydney with its northern suburbs is no subtle endeavour on the part of a certain section of the community with the proverbial axe to grind to enrich themselves at the public expense … The question is one of national importance since it follows that the benefits received by the metropolis extend far beyond its area, just as improvement in the country produces a corresponding effect upon the city.

By using the rhetoric of national development and 'public necessity' the League, dominated by lower North Shore interests, hoped to quash the oft-mooted possibility that at least some of the cost would be born by the ratepayers of the North Shore, just because they would be the most frequent users.

In the *Harbour Bridge Act* of 1922 not even the Nationalist government of the time was prepared to let the North Shore get off scot-free. Although the northern electorates had Nationalist members, they were relatively few compared to those to be found in the majority of electorates to the east, west and south of the city proper. The Act provided one-third of the capital cost – the cost of the roadway and footways on the Bridge and approaches – would be met by the owners of property in the City of Sydney, and to the north of the harbour the municipalities of North Sydney, Manly, Mosman, Lane Cove and Willoughby, the shires of Warringah and Ku-ring-gai, and part of the shire of Hornsby. The Act imposed a 'betterment tax' of a halfpenny in the pound (0.2 per cent) on the unimproved

capital value of the 'lands to be benefited'. At the time these 'lands' were seen to be most of the populated North Shore (but not as far west as Ryde) and the City of Sydney. Until well after World War II most Sydneysiders thought that the primary beneficiaries of the Bridge would be North Shore residents and city business people. Few foresaw that the Bridge would so integrate the two halves of the city that it would become a pivot for work, business, education, shopping and leisure trips from most parts of the metropolitan area.

The betterment tax, imposed from 1 January 1923 on the grounds that taxpayers would be saved the interest accrued during construction, was to be lifted about 15 years from that date. The 11 389 rateable properties in the City of Sydney were to pay an average of almost £7 each, while the 16 374 rateable properties in Warringah Shire were to pay less than 4 shillings each. Yet land speculators in Warringah were already trying to reap the benefits of the Bridge. In the early 1920s Willmore and Randell, young Sydney real estate agents, had to go further afield than the established agencies, who held the middle ring market. With a fleet of smart new Buicks to ferry prospective purchasers in, Willmore and Randell advertised 'beach-side estates' at Avalon, billed as 'closer than Cronulla' (a popular surfing resort south of Botany Bay):

> Far sighted people will buy NOW at Avalon, before the new road construction is completed next Summer. Avalon is only one hour's run from the heart of the City – closer than Cronulla. On completion of the North Shore Bridge, scores of people will make Avalon their permanent place of residence.

It is clear in retrospect that speculators in North Shore land had as much to gain from the Bridge – at

Sydney - A City Symphony 1932 — R Emerson Curtis

< In his 'Sydney: A City Symphony' 1932 Emerson Curtis captured the flavour of Sydney as both a working and a leisure city, the entire edifice held together by the Bridge at the top. The new underground railway whisks people around the city centre while the ocean liner provides the link to the wider world. Sydneysiders and visitors can hear orators at the Domain, go to the zoo or the beach. Sydney is presented as the surfing and film capital of Australia. Gouache, watercolour, and pencil on paper, Spearritt collection, Museum of Sydney

> The elegant art deco tramway bridge, itself supported by a mini arch, crossed the Bradfield Highway at the northern approaches. Department of Main Roads, c 1933

least in the short term – as city businesses. Indeed these apparently separate interests often turned out to be the same capitalists in a different guise. All the major real estate agencies – Raine and Horne, Richardson and Wrench, Hardie and Gorman, had headquarters in the city, but their principals often lived on the North Shore.

The city interests to benefit most obviously from the Bridge were the large retail emporiums: David Jones (which opened a store opposite the new St James Station in late 1926), Farmers (corner of George and Market Streets), Anthony Hordern (taking up a whole city block between Pitt and George Streets) and to a lesser degree Grace Brothers (its Broadway store was too far from the central business district for the Bridge to be of more than an indirect benefit).

Ratepayers in Manly, Lane Cove, Mosman, North Sydney, Willoughby, Hornsby and Ku-ring-gai were to pay additional rates of between 7 shillings and 15 shillings per annum, a lot less than the amount asked of city ratepayers. Within

the city centre there were even more dramatic differences in the unimproved capital value of the land, from the huge sites held by retail, insurance, import, export and banking interests to the tiny tenanted terraces on the outskirts of the central city, where it was not directly the tenants but the landlords who would be paying the betterment tax.

The *Bridge Act* provided that the Railway Commissioners bear the other two thirds of the cost. They were to have four railway lines, two on the western side of the Bridge to connect with the already existing North Shore line to Hornsby and two on the eastern side to connect the city with Bradfield's proposed railway line through Mosman and Manly to Narrabeen. The Commissioners estimated that their profit from train travellers after paying interest and working expenses would be over £250 000 in the Bridge's first year of operation.

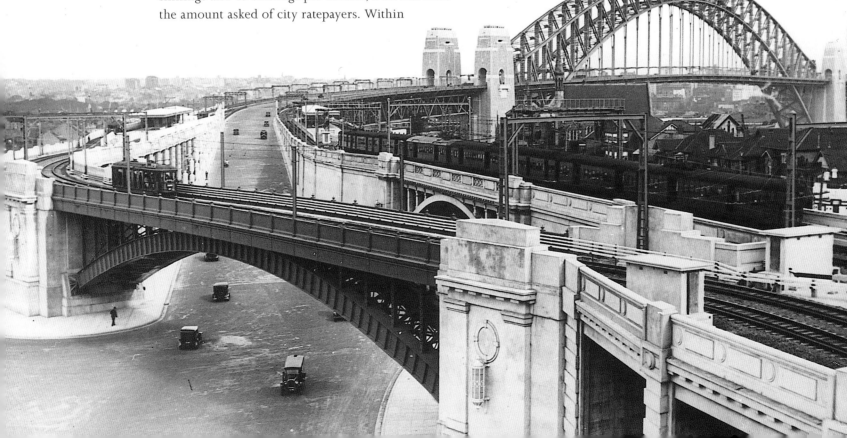

In 1922 the Railway Commissioners readily agreed to let the tramways use the two tracks on the eastern side of the Bridge, at least until their own northern beaches railway was built. By the late 1920s they were having second thoughts, because although they saw little chance of starting work on that railway line, they could see that handing over two tracks to the tramway might postpone the railway even further. The tramways did end up getting government permission to use the two tracks and, in the 1930s, served the lower North Shore, Manly and Narrabeen. In December 1932 the State government, in an attempt to counter the competition of private bus operators, established its own bus services, and in August 1937 State bus services were extended across the Bridge. It was the thin end of the wedge. Two years later the 14-kilometre tramline from the Spit to Manly and Narrabeen was replaced by a bus service. Trams continued to service the lower North Shore providing a direct link to the city. But the Railway Commissioners were no nearer to getting their cherished northern suburbs line which Bradfield had so forcefully advocated in his 1925 report. They had lost the battle. Trams continued to use the Bridge until June 1958, when the rail beds were converted to roadways to meet the insatiable demands of motorists and truck drivers. Rail freight, following the suburbanisation of manufacturing from the 1950s, simply could not compete with the truck as a means of moving raw materials, goods and equipment from one part of the metropolis to another.

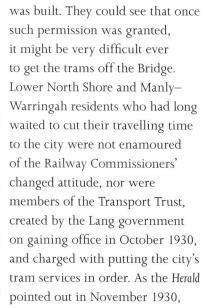

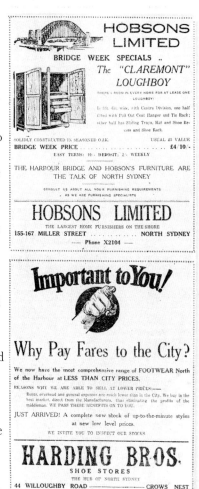

Even before the Bridge opened the Railway Commissioners had begun to have reservations about their original agreement to let the tramways use the two eastern tracks until the northern suburbs railway was built. They could see that once such permission was granted, it might be very difficult ever to get the trams off the Bridge. Lower North Shore and Manly–Warringah residents who had long waited to cut their travelling time to the city were not enamoured of the Railway Commissioners' changed attitude, nor were members of the Transport Trust, created by the Lang government on gaining office in October 1930, and charged with putting the city's tram services in order. As the *Herald* pointed out in November 1930,

North Shore ratepayers have now been paying the special bridge rate for eight years, in the belief that the Bridge will bring them immediately into unbroken contact with the city. Indications that this will not be accomplished, as far as large numbers are concerned, are already provoking strong protests and considerable indignation … The Transport Trust may be expected to put up a sturdy fight for trams on the bridge. If North Shore trams are not given permission to cross, an awkward situation is likely to arise. The public will chafe at the suggestion that they should have to change from trams at the North Shore stations merely to climb into electric trains for the brief journey to the city [27 November 1930].

> The Commissioner for Railways happily appropriated the style of the London Underground in publicising the 'Sydney Suburban and City Underground Railway'. The top map graphically outlines the entire suburban electric system, while the underground map shows the Circular Quay line still to be completed. It didn't open until 1956. Railway map, 1939. Spearritt collection

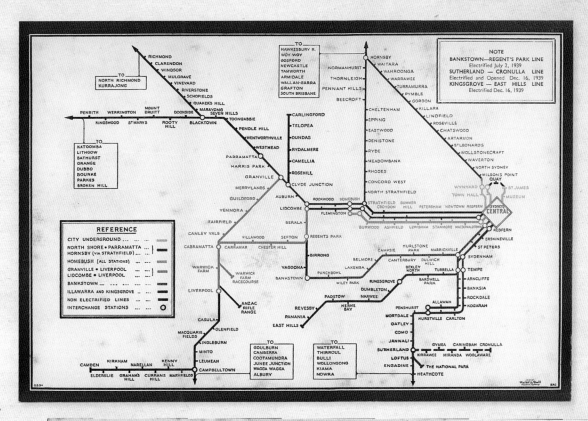

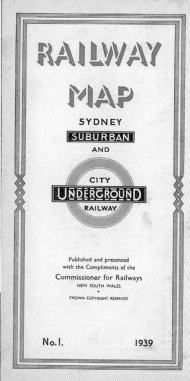

The Bridge toll

Ever since the 'betterment tax' was levied on the City of Sydney and North Shore municipalities in 1923, some businessmen had railed against it and advocated the introduction of a toll. In April 1931 the Taxpayers Association of New South Wales provided articles for the *Sydney Morning Herald* and the *Daily Telegraph* on the need for a toll. The articles were then republished in booklet form. The Association, which included among its members the former Nationalist Premier Sir Benjamin Fuller and the leading city retailer Charles Lloyd Jones, had as its object the reduction of all forms of taxation. The articles and the booklet were written by one of its members, Alderman AE Norden of North Sydney Council.

Norden pointed out that despite the contract price of £4 200 000 the Bridge and approaches were likely to cost over £8 million. By April 1931 somewhat over £1 million had been collected by the municipalities, leaving over £1.5 million still to be collected. He went on to argue:

> On present real estate values, in view of the depression, it will probably take a further 12 to 15 years for the municipalities to fully pay their quota ... Many taxpayers will derive no personal benefit in the use of the bridge. For instance, residents of Mosman, Neutral Bay, and Cremorne, south of Military Road, will continue to use the ferries ... The owners of property in the city area, generally speaking, may likewise be deemed to have derived no greater advantage than will accrue to those municipalities contiguous to the city which are exempt from the payment of the rate.

Norden wanted the users to contribute towards the cost, partly because he decried the 'craze for free service' and partly because he wanted to reduce the burden on ratepayers and taxpayers 'suffering' in the Depression. He even argued that pedestrians should pay a toll. The financial plight of tenants in the city or the lower North Shore who might need to use the Bridge was of no interest to the Taxpayers Association.

The Taxpayers Association soon won the support of the Graziers Association, who argued that the property owners who had already paid large sums in Bridge taxes should be recompensed from the toll. The toll also won support from the ruling right-wing alliance in the City Council, who suggested that the recession in retailing and building was burden enough on city taxpayers. Labor members on Council opposed the toll on the grounds that businessmen would gain most from the Bridge and should therefore bear the cost. Opposition came also from a public meeting at North Sydney in October 1931, where Alderman Primrose (a colleague of Norden's on the North Sydney Council) argued that a toll would be unfair to 'residents' as distinct from ratepayers on the north side and that more municipalities should be subject to the special tax.

The Lang government, elected in October 1930, agreed to introduce a toll. It may be that the Labor Party thought that the bulk of the toll would come from the middle- and upper-class ratepayers on the North Shore, but in that case the Party was forgetting that 70 per cent of the residents of North Shore were at that time tenants, many of whom worked in the city or adjacent industrial areas. Indeed North Sydney actually had, from October 1930 to May 1932 a Labor member, Benjamin Howe, who, with his wife, ran a soup kitchen for the poor of the municipality. On the other side of the harbour, in the city municipality, the proportion of residents who were tenants was only a little lower than in North Sydney. Certainly

> Photographer David Moore captures the morning peak hour traffic in Sydney in 1947. There are five lanes of traffic going into the city and only one going out. At the time most white collar jobs were still in the city centre, which also dominated the retail trade. Most industrial jobs were in the inner western and southern suburbs. Despite the obvious congestion, in 1947 trains and trams still carried more people over the Bridge than motor vehicles. 'Sydney Harbour II, 1947'

fewer of them needed to come to the north side for jobs, but many looked forward to be able to get a tram to the northern beaches, and even to go camping at Narrabeen. Only when one got to the secluded middle-class municipality of Ku-ring-gai were a majority of the residents home owners and ratepayers. The betterment tax on North Shore ratepayers and city businesses was not abolished until 1937, when a sympathetic non-Labor government let the Taxpayers Association have its way.

Once a toll was decided on, further controversy ensued about who would pay it. A month before the Bridge opening, Lang announced, in a popular move, that no charge would be made for pedestrians. Motorists had to wait until three days before the opening to be

The Toll Spider's Web.

< The *Smiths Weekly* cartoon, 19 March 1932, captured the popular attitude of the time with 'the Toll Spider's web'. The Bridge remains the longest-standing tolled structure in Australia

∨ Toll collectors had to wait some years to get enclosed toll structures. In Depression Sydney car ownership and car usage fell, and for most of its span the Bridge only had one marked line down the middle. State Records New South Wales NRS12685, 1933

> In marketing Sydney, ferries play the role of trams in Melbourne. The 'freedom of Sydney harbour' came at a modest price. The Bridge quickly assumed centre stage in all Sydney tourist promotions from the mid-1920s. Brochure c 1938

told that drivers would be charged 6 pence each, plus 3 pence for any other adults in the car and 1 pence for children. This well-timed announcement muted criticism of the toll, the issue swamped in the euphoria of the opening ceremonies. The full list of charges is indicative of the remarkable variety of vehicles using the Bridge:

> Motor cars and motor cycles with side-cars attached, 6d each. Bicycles, tricycles, and motor cycles without side car, 3d each. Sulkies and four wheeled buggies and light carts, 3d each. Vans, lorries, drays, wagons, the tare weight of which does not exceed 2 tons, 1 shilling each, between two and three tons 2 shillings each, over 3 tons 3 shillings each. Horse and rider 3d. Horses or cattle (loose stock), per head, 2d. Sheep or pigs, per head, 1d.

Charging such a relatively high sum for a car driver with no passengers (6 pence in 1932 is now equivalent to about $5 in buying power) was a relatively easy move for a Labor government. In the interwar years cars were almost entirely the preserve of the middle class, and especially so in the midst of the Depression. Charging 3 pence for bicycles and motor cycles was a little steep, but the charges did not deter the populace when the toll first came into effect on midnight of 19 March 1932, after a day of celebrations. That Sunday 21 000 motor vehicles containing more than 80 000 passengers passed over the Bridge, almost four occupants per vehicle. In 2005 the average occupancy per vehicle was 1.2.

FREEDOM of SYDNEY HARBOUR
AVAILABLE 7 DAYS 5'

Ask for a VISITORS HARBOUR CONCESSION TICKET

1 MANLY BEACH and Return

2 TARONGA ZOO PARK Return Ferry Trip and Admission

3 SHOWBOAT HARBOUR CRUISE Morning or Afternoon Trip

4 LUNA PARK (Milsons Pt.) Season Oct. to June Free Admission and Return Ferry Trip.

5 SEVEN DAYS' FREE FERRY TRAVEL on Services of Sydney Ferries Limited

> A typical decorative spoon of the era, often sold in sets of two or four. Spearritt collection

117

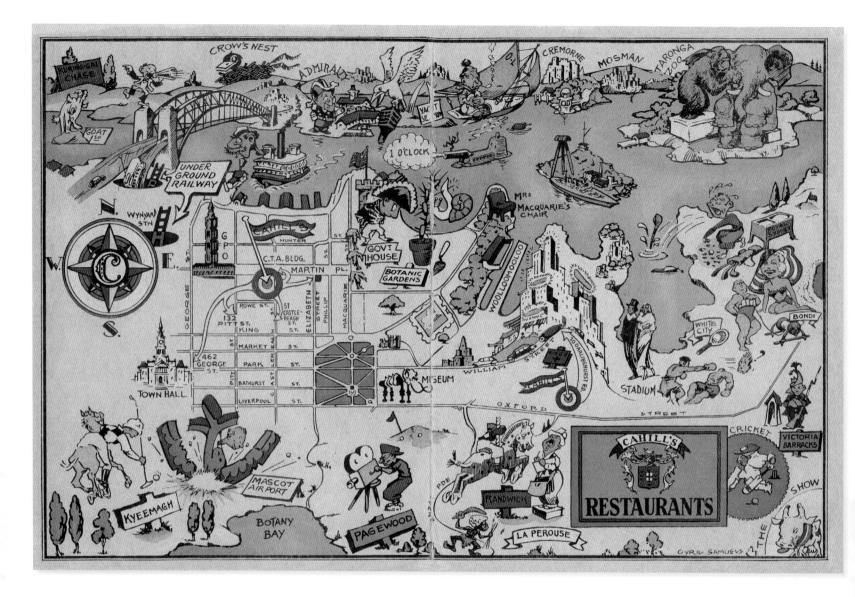

Who crosses the Bridge?

The Bridge spans the entire history of modern Australian transport. In the early years, the Main Roads Board (later to be called the Department of Main Roads (DMR)) collected statistics on all crossings, even those by pedestrians, cyclists and horse-drawn vehicles. As the Bridge opened at the end of the horse-drawn era, such detailed statistics were not kept for long.

Of the 2 193 082 people who crossed the Bridge in motor vehicles, only 6.5 per cent were children. Well off North Shore people drove to their city offices, where car parks were replacing stables. Most other motorists on the Bridge were truck drivers, delivery men and tradesmen. Only a tiny proportion of women held licences and children walked, cycled or got public transport to school. The daily average in October 1932 for car passengers and drivers was 20 000 while for pedestrians it was 4500. In the depressed conditions of the time, many walked not

PASSENGER TRAFFIC ACROSS THE BRIDGE ROADWAY
March to October 1932

38 85	Motor cycles with side cars
257 499	Bicycles, motorcycles, sulkies*
130 224	Lorries
1 966 508	Motor cars
718	Loose stock

*Two-wheeled one-horse vehicles

< The Cahill's Restaurant group distributed this map to market their growing chain of eating establishments. Trams can be seen disappearing off the Bridge into the tram tunnels. Like a lot of Sydney iconography of the 1950s this map emphasises the range of leisure activities and locations in Sydney. Map c 1950, Spearritt collection

for the view or exercise, but to save money on the way to work or to look for work.

Learning to use the Bridge was no easy matter. Sydney motorists had never been presented with such a lavish section of 'highway'. In September 1932, just five months after the Bridge was opened, two traffic policemen were killed and the Commissioner of Police complained about the tendency for drivers of motor vehicles to admire the scenery on each side of the Bridge when crossing it rather than to give undivided attention to the roadway in front. He also complained that some motorists were using the Bridge as a speedway and he asked the Public Works Department to paint a white line down the centre

of the roadway. At that time and for a long time afterwards there were in effect only two very wide lanes across the Bridge, though traffic was expected to form two lines in the northbound lane and two lines in the south. The toll stands, open to the weather, were at the southern end of the Bridge.

Changing patronage patterns on the Bridge are shown in the accompanying graph which provides transport information unique in Australia. Despite the gradual growth of car ownership in the 1930s, rail tram and bus travellers accounted for more than two-thirds of all crossings throughout that decade. Tram numbers were helped by a reduction in the adult fare of 4 pence to 3 pence in October 1932 and 2 pence in January 1938. In that year the fare for children was

ᐯ Toll booths on the southern side c 1952, with double decker buses in the background. Department of Main Roads

reduced from 2 pence to 1 pence. In the previous year both private and government buses were allowed to extend their services across the Bridge, thereby breaking the monopoly that the tramways and railway had previously enjoyed. The introduction of petrol rationing during World War II so cut road traffic on the Bridge that there were calls in October 1941 for an increase in the toll to cover a likely deficit in Bridge repayments. The *Sydney Morning Herald*, regarded by many Labor supporters as the house journal of the bourgeoisie, attacked this move in a pointed editorial:

> Petrol rationing, together with the high cost of the spirit, has driven many motor vehicles off the roads … increased bridge tolls would accelerate the present tendency to lay up cars and trucks. The bridge tolls are already high

The systematic abolition of trams in Sydney from the early 1950s coincided with a spectacular increase in car ownership, from 95 vehicles per 1000 people in 1943 (the low point during the war) to 196 vehicles in 1953. By June 1959, when the two tram tracks were converted to roadway, vehicle numbers had reached 270 per 1000 people. That year was the first time that private vehicles accounted for more passenger trips over the Bridge than the combined public transport services. For a number of reasons it seems likely that the Bridge changeover may have come before that for the city as a whole. Car ownership was higher to the north of the harbour than elsewhere in Sydney because of the greater wealth of the middle-class suburbs and because new areas of development in parts of Hornsby, Ku-ring-gai and Warringah were not served by public transport. As Sydney grew well beyond its rail and bus routes, many new developments – from hospitals and universities to shopping centres and factories – assumed that their workers would drive. More and more women not only passed their driving tests but purchased cars of their own.

The spectacular rise in road patronage on the Bridge was little remarked on at the time because motor cars were now seen as an integral part of everyday life, but the growing congestion posed problems for the DMR. The capacity of the 17-metre roadway was increased to three rather narrow lanes in each direction and by 1949 the reverse lanes arrangement had been introduced whereby four lanes were used for traffic flow in the peak direction. A decade later, when the DMR converted the two abandoned tram tracks to road lanes, there were eight narrow lanes for traffic. An equally dramatic change, also designed to speed traffic flow, came in July 1970 when the one-way toll was introduced. Tolls were now only paid by southbound traffic, though motorists using the Cahill Expressway still paid their toll at the northern end. (The Cahill Expressway, completed in 1958, comprised a roadway above Circular Quay Station, opened two years earlier.) The toll, which by 1966 on the introduction of decimalisation stood at 1 shilling, was doubled in 1970 to 20 cents.

Twenty cents in 1970 (and a mere 40 cents for lorries over 2 tonnes) was far less that the 6 pence per car and 3 pence per passenger of the 1930s, but the increase still caused a minor outcry and for a while a number of motorists were said to be going out of their way to use the Gladesville Bridge, completed in 1964. The DMR hoped that the Gladesville Bridge, which it claimed as the longest span concrete arch in the world, would take the pressure off the Harbour Bridge. And indeed for a little while this seemed to be the case, but car ownership and usage continued to grow at such a pace that the relief proved short-lived.

> Peak hour traffic arrangements in the early 1960s before the building of the Warringah Expressway. As this map makes plain, North Sydney became a major congestion point in both the morning and afternoon peak periods. With the rapid growth of car ownership in the 1950s and 1960s more and more people drove to work. Map c 1964, Spearritt collection

∧ Toll tokens were in use on the Bridge from the 1930s to the 1980s and could be bought in multiples to save motorists time. They are now actively traded on eBay

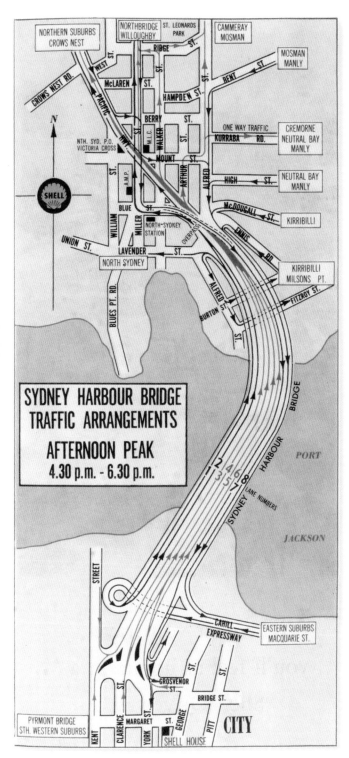

SYDNEY HARBOUR BRIDGE TRAFFIC ARRANGEMENTS

AFTERNOON PEAK
4.30 p.m. – 6.30 p.m.

^ Motoring on the Bridge in 1979, with signage above the roadway instructing drivers on toll charges. Kodachrome slide, Jill Abbott, 1979

The toll continued to come to public attention. In 1977 a *Sydney Morning Herald* editorial asked, 'Why are the residents of Hobart sweeping happily across their new bridge without having to grope in their pockets? Because Canberra gave the money for their bridge. We're still paying for ours.' A few months later the pro-public transport Australian Transport Study Group advocated increasing the toll to 50 cents to discourage people from taking their cars into the city. The NRMA – one of the principal lobby groups responsible for the abolition of the trams – which claimed to represent 1.5 million New South Wales motorists, said that the suggestion was 'totally unrealistic'. Two years later the first female toll collectors were appointed, an event which just a few years before would also have been decried as totally unrealistic.

The Bridge toll now receives much less public scrutiny because in the last 25 years toll roads have become common. Brisbane opened its Gateway toll bridge in 1986, directly linking the Gold Coast to the Sunshine Coast. Melbourne embarked on a grand tollway system, with electronic tolling, in the mid-1990s, while most of Sydney's recent motorways are also tollways. The tollways mainly attract public criticism if they become congested or conversely, underused. When the cross city tunnel tollway opened in Sydney in 2005, the State government attempted to ensure its commercial success for its private owners by closing many city streets. The tollway didn't attract the predicted daily usage and such was the public outcry over the road closures that most were reversed in 2006.

The Bridge and the Warringah Expressway (surplus toll moneys were used to acquire property for its construction in the mid 1960s) remain firmly in public hands. But the Sydney Harbour Tunnel, like the new motorways, only came to fruition as a privately financed venture.

> Electronic indicators were installed above lanes in the 1990s. In this morning peak photograph by Michael Perini (2006), buses ply their dedicated bus lane offering much quicker travel times than cars from the North Shore to the city. Double decker trains have proved very effective in moving large numbers of passengers at peak hour

> Data on Sydney Harbour Bridge crossings is unique in Australia, enabling us to compare public transport and private motor vehicle use over 80 years. Private vehicle growth has slowed and trains are at capacity during peak hour. Only buses have seen a substantial increase in both crossings and passengers, up twenty per cent from 2007 to 2010. At peak hour buses carry more than one and a half times as many people as private motor vehicles. Sources: NSW Government Yearbooks, plus data from RTA, Rail Corp and the State Transport Authority

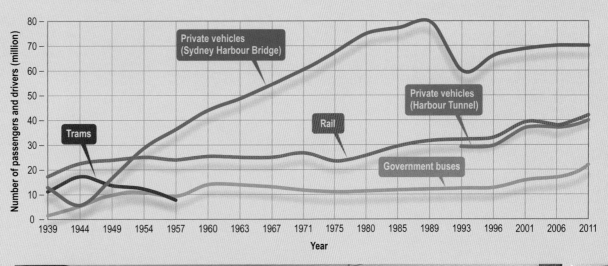

^ Sydney remains a topographically complex city. In the late 1980s the Department of Main Roads (which became the Road Traffic Authority in a merger with the Department of Motor Transport in 1989) published its plan *Roads 2000*. Such plans were predicated on an exponential increase in road usage, and that was certainly the case from the late 1940s to the 1990s.

> Traffic monitoring has a long history. 'Inside the nerve centre of the Sydney Harbour Bridge' In 1980 traffic was monitored on 12 TV screens. Fairfax photo

SYDNEY HARBOUR SUNSHINE TOURS

10 DAYS' HOLIDAY
FOR £14-14-0
17 DAYS FOR £18-18-0

Including
FIRST CLASS RETURN RAIL TRAVEL
FIRST CLASS HOTEL ACCOMMODATION
TAXI TRANSPORT TO AND FROM HOTEL
HARBOUR CRUISES . . . . MOTOR TOURS

UNDER DIRECTION OF SYDNEY FERRIES LTD.
in Association with

VICTORIAN GOVT. TOURIST BUREAU
Queen's Walk, Melbourne, and at Spencer Street Station

ASK FOR FREE BOOKLET

^ Sydney Ferries and the
Victorian Government
Tourist Bureau luring
Melburnians to Sydney
in the late 1930s. Poster,
State Library of Victoria

WHY THIS CAN'T HAPPEN

When Steel Grows Tired. Why is it possible to assert that great steel structures will not collapse? Because the strength of steel may be calculated with scientific accuracy. Steel is a combination of iron and carbon, the hardness of which is determined by chemical content and internal structure of metal.

Fatigue in steel is a condition in which the microscopic crystals of which it is composed readjust themselves and produce condition of brittleness. Gentle tapping may produce this "fatigue," while great strain will leave the metal unaffected. Overheating of steel will burn out carbon content and render metal useless. Steel of Sydney Harbor Bridge was tested by Testing Branch of Public Works Department until complet.on of structure. All cement manufactured in N.S.W. is also tested by this department before manufacture.

How Sydney got a harbour tunnel

In 1964 the State Opposition leader Robin Askin,
in a determined bid for office, promised a tunnel
or a second bridge if the Liberals were elected. This
election promise, like that of Sir Henry Parkes, over
seven decades before, was soon forgotten, although
the Liberals managed to hold onto power until Labor
won under Neville Wran in 1976. In 1980 Premier
Wran stated that he thought work on a tunnel should
begin within three years. As the up-market *Sydney City
Monthly*, a local imitation of lavish American lifestyle
magazines, commented in March 1981,

> Sydney has more cross-harbour tunnel schemes
> than pigeonholes to put them in. None ever broke
> the bureaucratic slumber … Politics being what it
> is, an alternative to the Harbour Bridge would have
> been built years ago if northern suburbs votes had
> been vital. They haven't been – to Labor or Liberal
> Governments. The Liberals have always been able
> to count on the shore, which is why they've never
> tried particularly hard to woo its voters either …
> The more cynical political observers suggest he
> [Wran] brought up the idea only because he had

been off the newspaper front pages for a few days.
Talk of harbour tunnels is guaranteed to make big,
bold headlines.

Tom Uren, Commonwealth Labor spokesman for
urban and regional affairs and member of the
western suburbs seat of Reid, bitterly attacked any
second crossing proposal:

> What it may be – a tunnel or a second harbour
> bridge – and wherever it may be, at this stage
> the construction of a second harbour crossing
> is against the interests of the great majority of
> the people of Sydney. There is already in Sydney
> Metropolitan area a gross imbalance in the
> provision of urban services. The eastern and
> northern suburbs are relatively well serviced,
> while the rapidly growing western and south-
> western corridors lack many vital services and
> social amenities [SMH, 14 February 1981].

When the normally dour DMR allowed the Bridge
to be closed to traffic for four hours on Sunday 21
March 1982 for the 50th anniversary celebrations,
they anticipated 50 000, but instead celebrants just
kept coming. Journalists estimated up to 500 000
people braved intermittent rain to swarm across the
roadway from both the southern and the northern
sides. So great were the crowds, especially when
they met in the middle of the Bridge, that the DMR
suggested some mounted police might assist with
crowd control. The DMR was also surprised at the
extent of public opposition to its proposal to add a
ninth lane to the Bridge, though readily achievable
in engineering terms. The opponents combined
a fear about Sydney being further overrun by
traffic with a new-found heritage and aesthetic
consciousness in Sydney about the importance of
the Bridge as the city's greatest structure.

In the 1980s Sydney's traffic problems
worsened, especially from the northern beaches,
where the only way into or across the city was

< Over a quarter of a
million people crossed the
Harbour Bridge for its 50th
anniversary in 1982, the first
time that the roadway had
been open to the people since
the opening in 1932. Neither
overcast weather nor rain
could dissuade enthusiastic
Sydneysiders from reclaiming
the Bridge. Neutral Bay
residents protested against
the 9th lane, then being
proposed by the Department
of Main Roads. Street parties
and fairs were held in a
number of locations,
including Observatory Hill.
Kodachrome transparencies,
Peter Spearritt, Sunday
21 March 1982

> Front cover of a real estate brochure, produced in 1928. This real estate company persisted in calling the Bridge, 'The North Shore Bridge', because it wanted to emphasise the boon that the Bridge would be for its land sale of 1000 blocks at Newport. Prospective purchasers were told that Newport, with an electric railway as per Dr Bradfield's plan, would be just 35 minutes from the city and that the blocks could well increase in value by 300 to 400 per cent, as had blocks near other Sydney beaches. The brochure depicts both electric trains, far left, and trams abutting them, though the tram tracks ended up on the eastern side, originally planned for rail. The northern beaches still await any form of public transport – whether rail or tram – that has its own right of way. Spearritt collection

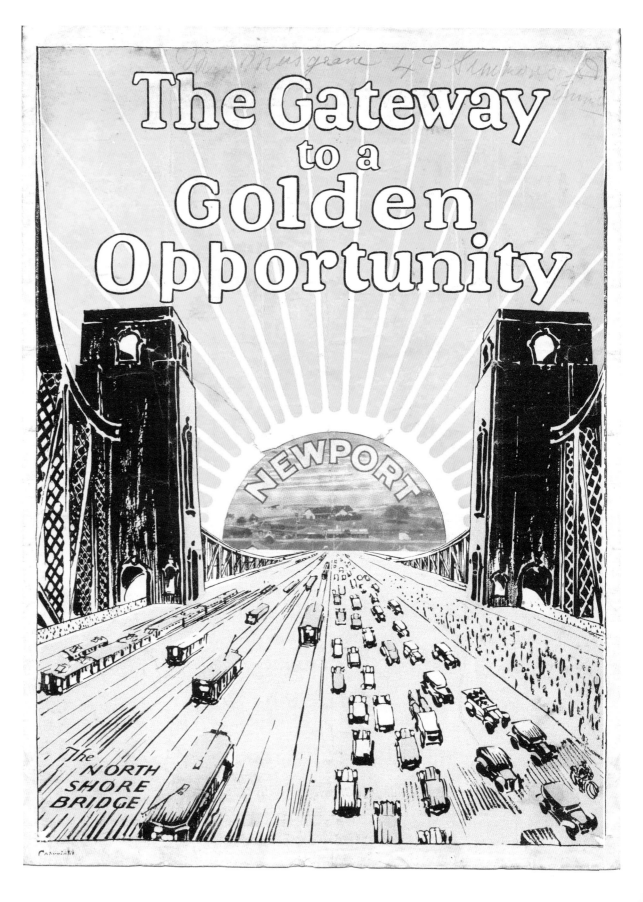

THE BALLAD OF THE BRIDGE

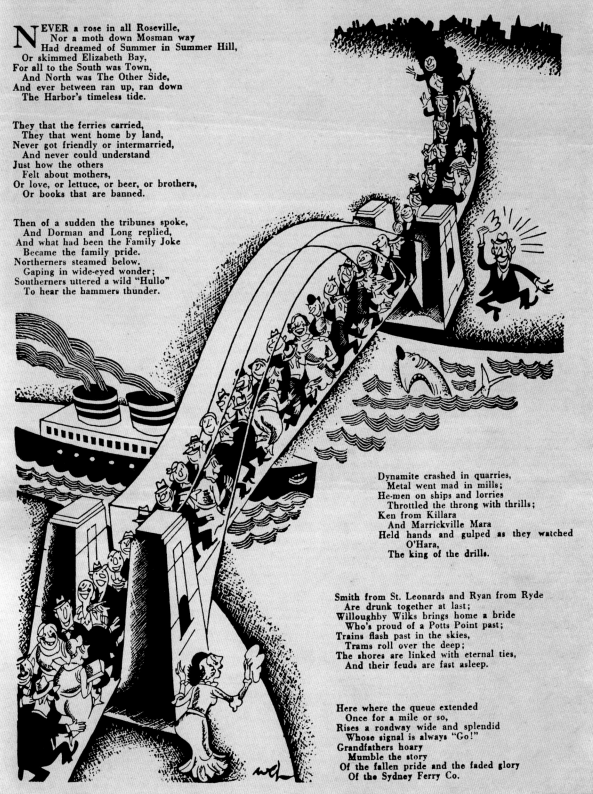

NEVER a rose in all Roseville,
    Nor a moth down Mosman way
  Had dreamed of Summer in Summer Hill,
  Or skimmed Elizabeth Bay,
For all to the South was Town,
    And North was The Other Side,
And ever between ran up, ran down
  The Harbor's timeless tide.

They that the ferries carried,
    They that went home by land,
Never got friendly or intermarried,
    And never could understand
Just how the others
    Felt about mothers,
Or love, or lettuce, or beer, or brothers,
    Or books that are banned.

Then of a sudden the tribunes spoke,
    And Dorman and Long replied,
And what had been the Family Joke
    Became the family pride.
Northerners steamed below.
    Gaping in wide-eyed wonder;
Southerners uttered a wild "Hullo"
    To hear the hammers thunder.

Dynamite crashed in quarries,
    Metal went mad in mills;
He-men on ships and lorries
    Throttled the throng with thrills;
Ken from Killara
    And Marrickville Mara
Held hands and gulped as they watched
    O'Hara,
    The king of the drills.

Smith from St. Leonards and Ryan from Ryde
    Are drunk together at last;
Willoughby Wilks brings home a bride
    Who's proud of a Potts Point past;
Trains flash past in the skies,
    Trams roll over the deep;
The shores are linked with eternal ties,
    And their feuds are fast asleep.

Here where the queue extended
    Once for a mile or so,
Rises a roadway wide and splendid
    Whose signal is always "Go!"
Grandfathers hoary
    Mumble the story
Of the fallen pride and the faded glory
    Of the Sydney Ferry Co.

< This image, drawn by 'wep' [William Edwin Pidgeon] with accompanying poem by Colin Wills, appeared in their book *Rhymes of Sydney*, an exuberant memento published in Sydney in 1933, in the midst of the Depression. Wills, a poet and a journalist, had a fine sense of the class structure of Sydney, as can be seen in the suburban references in the poem, which he ends with a comment about 'the faded glory of the Sydney Ferry Co.'. Bill Pidgeon, a painter and cartoonist, who later went on to win the Archibald Prize, had a close knowledge and a great fondness for Sydney's characters. The image originally appeared in black and white. *Rhymes of Sydney*, (Johnson, Sydney, 1933; later republished by Pylon Press, Sydney, 1982)

127

by bus or private car, in both cases using choked roads. In the morning and evening peak hours the ten lanes of the Warringah Expressway had to feed into many fewer lanes to get onto the Bridge. Engineering companies plotted lucrative solutions to exponential traffic growth, as they still do today. Residents of Greenwich (west of the Bridge on the northern side) and Balmain (west of the Bridge on the southern side) bitterly opposed a tunnel, one of four proposals unveiled in December 1981. They joined hands of protest across the Harbour with their Combined Bridge Action Group. By 1981 Balmain's industries were being replaced by middle class residents while Greenwich was losing its industrial demeanour, so powerful professional groups were at work. Such a Bridge crossing would have met much less effective protest in the 1920s.

Wargon Chapman Partners saw that a tunnel could utilise the existing Warringah and Cahill Expressway lanes without entailing any of the demolition and property resumptions that dogged each and every possible Bridge route. In 1984 the engineers approached the Australian construction company Transfield and the Japanese firm Kumagai Gumi, leaders in immersed tube tunnelling. These two firms, then working on a ski tube tunnel in the Perisher Valley in the Snowy Mountains, formed a joint venture with the Westpac bank to suggest ways of financing the project.

The immersed tube tunnel still required dredging a trench in the harbour floor and environment groups expressed concern about the amount of sediment dislodged. They were even more alarmed, as was the North Sydney Council, that the two northern pylons would be commandeered as giant ventilation vents to expel foul tunnel air, fresh air being sucked in from a huge intake vent at ground level near the north-east pylon.

The tunnel consortium managed to keep the

lid on environmental protests by a clever public relations campaign on the theme 'Now you see it … Now you don't', showing pictures of maritime construction and tunnelling and the final result: the entire tunnel edifice covered by the tranquil waters of the harbour. Using the northern pylons as exhaust pipes meant that the consortium could avoid any ugly vertical structure that might have given environmentalists something to 'hang' their campaign on. The tunnel proponents were quick to claim that 800 buildings had been demolished for the Harbour Bridge while none would be demolished for their tunnel.

Construction began in January 1988, the start of the Bicentennial year and the tunnel opened on 31 August 1992. Over 4500 people worked on the 2.3 kilometre tunnel with a peak work force of 800 at any one time. The eight tunnel segments for the 1 kilometre that is under-water, were constructed at Port Kembla and towed up the coast and into Sydney Harbour. But because most of the activity involved relatively discrete tunnelling on both sides of the harbour and immersing the tunnel segments

^ Sydney cartoonist Benier's comment on the Harbour Tunnel in the NRMA magazine *The Open Road*. Many people still choose to drive over the Bridge because of the vistas and a sense of engineering wonder. The Harbour Tunnel offers no such vistas, hence Benier's suggestion to appropriate marine life from the Sydney Aquarium. April 1989

the construction didn't attract a great deal of public attention. It had none of the drama of the building of the Bridge.

The opening of the Sydney Harbour Tunnel proved to be a tawdry occasion, sponsored by the now defunct Advance Bank and the cosmetics firm Nutrimetics, who had signs informing those of us who walked through it on the day how far we were below the harbour surface. Walking in a tunnel built into a trench on the harbour floor had none of the grandeur of either the Harbour Bridge opening in 1932 or subsequent Bridge closures, where pedestrians take over the Bridge roadway usually as a celebration of both the structure and the city or in the case of the reconciliation march in 2000, as a public statement.

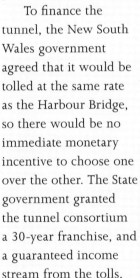

> The Sydney Harbour Tunnel is administered from the white building in the top right of this photograph, which shows Warringah Expressway lanes feeding into the northern approaches to the tunnel. Photograph by John Storey, September 2006

To finance the tunnel, the New South Wales government agreed that it would be tolled at the same rate as the Harbour Bridge, so there would be no immediate monetary incentive to choose one over the other. The State government granted the tunnel consortium a 30-year franchise, and a guaranteed income stream from the tolls, which would pay for the construction cost of $560 million, financing costs and give a handsome profit. The tunnel is due to be handed back to the government in 2022.

In its first years of operation the tunnel caused a significant dip in Harbour Bridge crossings, but by 2010 the Bridge, at 166 000 daily vehicle crossings, had almost got back to its pre-tunnel daily average (see graph p 123). This demonstrates the well known transport truism that traffic increases to match roadway capacity. In 2005 the tunnel carried 86 000 vehicles per day, similar to the numbers carried on the Gladesville, Tom Ugly's and Ryde bridges. Only the Anzac Bridge, a striking suspension bridge opened in 1995 (originally called the Glebe Island Bridge) and carrying 129 000 vehicles per day by 2005, got anywhere near the Harbour Bridge traffic levels. And none of these other structures carry trains, which account for 104 000 passengers per day, while buses carry 60 000 passengers per day.

Cashless tolling came to the harbour tunnel in 2007 and to the Bridge in 2010, marking the end of 78 years of toll keepers. Time-of-day tolling, introduced to both the tunnel and the Bridge in 2009, makes it more expensive to travel at peak hour.

With the continuing decline in the world's oil reserves and steep increases in the price of petrol it is quite possible that the mix between public and private transport on the Sydney Harbour Bridge could change in favour of public transport. The two abandoned tram lanes (one of which is now a dedicated bus lane) could easily be given over to light rail, the only way the northern beach suburbs will ever get efficient links to the city centre.

Steel symphony

*The light was stronger now. You could see the red roofs
and the spires of the churches and the grey skyline of the city.
You could see the dome of the Zoo on the opposite hillcrest,
and the great, ghostly arc of the bridge ... Oliver looked up
at the sky. It was ridged with flame which faded as he watched.
The long waterway beneath lost itself in a western haze of paling
gold; the bridge spanned it like a rainbow, the city skyline
sank into a lavender-coloured mist.*

Sydney Bridge   Margaret Preston

< Margaret Preston captured the 19th century sensibility of Circular Quay and the Rocks in her *Sydney Bridge* 1932, black ink woodcut, hand coloured with gouche. Art Gallery of New South Wales

^ Sydney Harbour Bridge and West Circular Quay from Kyle House, 1931. Watercolour drawing by Sydney Ure Smith. National Gallery of Victoria

When Eleanor Dark used the Bridge in the opening and closing scenes of her novel *Waterway* (1938) she resisted the temptation to dwell on detail. Yet like many other writers and artists of her generation she did not – perhaps could not – ignore it.

The Bridge excited Sydney's poets, painters, novelists and photographers. When the elite magazine *Art in Australia* issued a 'Sydney Number' in June 1927 the harbour and the Bridge – the latter then but half-formed – were central concerns. Sydney Ure Smith and Leon Gellert wrote in their editorial:

> Hills, noise, traffic, narrow streets, careless pedestrians, yellow cabs, the harbour at night, ferries darting in a tangle into the harbour from Circular Quay. Tall buildings, ugly buildings, still more ugly buildings – incredibly ugly buildings – here and there a dignified structure.

Those artists who chose to portray the Bridge depicted it as a 'dignified structure', something to be treasured rather than satirised. The *Art in Australia* 'Sydney Number' included a nostalgic oil by Will Ashton called *The Last of Old Milson's Point*, a nostalgic reference to the changes that were about to take place there. Percy Lindsay's oil, *Building the North Shore Bridge*, took the opposite tack, depicting the inexorable advance of the approaches on the northern side of the harbour. As part of the adventurous modernism of the time *Art in Australia* also included photos by Harold Cazneaux, whose composition and tones were at once modern and romantic. His *Building the Harbour Bridge* showed the construction towers in sharp relief at Dawes Point while his *Sydney from Milson's Point* depicted the approaches in the early stages of construction and gave an observer a feeling for the enormous span of harbour that had to be crossed.

131

Photography as art

The Bridge attracted and entranced many notable
photographers, but none more than Harold
Cazneaux. In 1930 *Art in Australia* published
Cazneaux's *Bridge Book*, a volume of 25 generously-
proportioned photographs printed in sepia. The
titles of some of the photographs are indicative of
his approach, which both celebrated the Bridge as an
engineering achievement and romanticised its form.
The Weavers captured the creeper cranes weaving the
steel framework as they approached each other,
The Sweep of the Bridge depicted the underbelly of the
approaches as it 'curves out over the water'. *Shadows
of Steel* caught the 'pattern of light and shadows
presented by the constructional works at the rear of
the pylon', while *Taking Strain* showed the 128 erection
cables which held back the arch on each side of the
water. *The Arch in the Sky*, depicting the half-arches
shortly before closure, carried the caption:

> Modern man has looked up at the austere arch
> of steel in much the same way as his primitive
> forbears regarded the rainbow – as something
> that commanded his reverence and admiration
> with a promise of future blessings.

The book concluded with three photographs
showing the closure of the half-arches, entitled
Colossus, *The Complete Arch* and *Celebrations*, with the
Union Jack and the Australian flag atop the creeper
cranes as they met.

   As Leon Gellert wrote in his introduction to *The
Bridge Book*:

> There are many lovers of Sydney … who look
> upon this bridge of ours with resentment. Their
> acrimony has risen with the erection of each
> panel. It represents the intrusion of the age of
> steel and the passing of individuality … To these
> objectors the rising towers of the city, even to
> Darlinghurst, are the only answer. The skyscraper

^ Cazneaux *The Arch in
the Sky*, from Dawes Point,
The Bridge Book, 1930.

Cazneaux lived and
worked at Roseville, on
the North Shore. National

Library of Australia,
courtesy Cazneaux family

132

THE BRIDGE BOOK

THE BRIDGE BY MOONLIGHT

Published by ART IN AUSTRALIA LTD. **BY CAZNEAUX** PRICE ONE SHILLING

∧ Sydney Ure Smith's firm Art in Australia published *The Bridge Book* in 1930, with Cazneaux's photograph 'The Bridge by Moonlight' on the front cover

> Sydney Harbour and the Bridge were a symbolic departure point for great ocean liners. *The Bridge Book*, 1930, back cover

Gellert's prose and Cazneaux's photographs were a hymn of praise to modern engineering, underlaid by a quiet but forceful nationalism. Gellert imagined the visitor from abroad, far out at sea, seeing a 'dark crescent in the mists' and 'as vision grows and he passes under the arch itself he recognises with awe one of the modern wonders of the world'.

A 'modern wonder of the world' was certainly how many artists treated the Bridge. And in a city with a 46-metre height limit (150 feet) on buildings, the Bridge grew to dominate its landscape, not least because most of the nearby structures were wharves, not office or apartment blocks. As Jean Curlewis wrote in 'Sydney Number' of *Art in Australia*, in the breathless prose popular amongst the avant-garde at that time:

is almost upon us, and a few more years will find Sydney's architecture rivalling the height of its bridge.

And for those who would begin a quarrel on aesthetic grounds let it be understood that the engineer will be the architect of to-morrow. Perfect engineering, as a thing of beauty, survives by its very simplicity. There is no waste. It achieves its purpose by the shortest route, the finest materials, and absolute obedience to natural laws. The perfect work of engineering is a perfect object of art and as such will be recognised by the critics of the future.

THE NEW SYDNEY HARBOUR BRIDGE
THE GREATEST ARCH BRIDGE IN THE WORLD

Jazz. Traffic. Noise. Trams, ferry boats, trams. Sirens. Steel hammers clanging. Builders in the city. Building a bridge in the sea city. Thrust of girders, web of girders over the sea.

Amateur filmmakers documented the construction of the Bridge and quite a lot of construction footage survives. But the Bridge did not entice feature filmmakers until 1930 in the silent movie *The Cheaters*, where it was used to mark time spent in gaol by one of the major protagonists, with a 'before' shot of the unfinished Bridge and an 'after' shot with the arches joined. In following decades film makers used the Bridge as an instant image to denote Sydney.

The Bridge in curve

At the same time as Cazneaux and other members of the Sydney Camera Circle, including the French-born Henri Mallard, were busily photographing the Bridge from every angle and in every kind of light, Sydney's artists were also taking up the challenge. In 1930, Grace Cossington Smith, born in 1892, painted *The Bridge in Curve*, while a year later Roland Wakelin, five years older than Cossington Smith, painted *The Bridge Under Construction*. Of these two works, the art historian Ruth Brack has commented:

The Bridge in Curve is a homage to modern engineering: there is no human element of sculptural sense as in Wakelin's painting of the same subject. His *Bridge Under Construction* has a curving road with a lone figure directing the eye toward the distant Bridge. Attention focuses on the foreground elements of solid buildings, road and figure. In *The Bridge in Curve* by Cossington Smith nothing detracts from the echoing concentricity in the unfinished span where steel had yet to meet. The picture centres on the sunray effects of the strokes of paint arching across the sky ... The short, sharp strokes in the sky of *In-Curve* emphasise

> Grace Cossington Smith lived in Turramurra, not far from Cazneaux. *The bridge in-curve*, 1930, tempera on cardboard, National Gallery of Victoria

the latent energy that draws the one incomplete span towards the other. The eye moves with a rush along the Bridge up to the highest point between the two spans – a point which is vigorous and moving, but nevertheless a space ... Wakelin's Bridge is static, planar and not seen from the dramatic diagonal of Cossington Smith's.(*Studies in Australian Art* June 1978)

Ironically both of these paintings are to be found in the National Gallery of Victoria, reflecting the fact that in the interwar years that gallery had more money and was more adventurous in its acquisitions than the Art Gallery of New South Wales.

Dorrit Black was another who took up the challenge of the Bridge. In 1929 Adelaide-born Black came to Sydney after two years in London and Paris. The following year she was represented at an exhibition at the Macquarie Galleries along with some other 'Sydney modernists'. Of all Black's paintings the one to attract the most attention was *The Bridge* (1930). Ian North argues in his book on Black that the Bridge, 'widely seen as a symbol of new nationalism, was a favoured subject for artists at the time, and its "modernity" made it the perfect subject for the *avant-garde*'. Humphrey McQueen, in

his book *The Black Swan of Trespass* (1979), has a less
charitable explanation:

> Australia was free of the sunless caverns of northern
> hemisphere metropolises. And since our cities
> were flat and relatively open, it is hardly surprising
> that Australia produced so few poets and painters
> inspired by thrusting towers and rapid transits. That
> the Sydney Harbour Bridge attracted so many artists
> is a monument to the absence of other comparable
> subjects.

Whatever the explanation, the Bridge certainly evoked
some of the more adventurous paintings of the time.

After the opening

The Bridge continued to excite painters and photographers after the opening just as it had done during the construction. Many artists and photographers have employed the Bridge as a subject or motif in their work.

Studio Anna, c 1960

Whether they were drawn by the magic of the Bridge and its setting, or they felt that using the Bridge was part of an apprenticeship that all artists in Sydney were somehow obliged to participate in, is difficult to say. Adelaide-born Margaret Preston, who had lived in Mosman since 1920, wrote of the Bridge in 1932 as one of 'the finest specimens of Meccano in the world', indicating 'the worship of the iron bound realism that has ruled the art of Australia generally'.

After the opening much of the Bridge photography stressed not just its form, but its utility, for the obvious reason that it was by then a working structure. During its construction photographer Henri Mallard had gone to great lengths to photograph the men at work, often to breathtaking backdrops. Most of Cazneaux's photographs, preoccupied with form, were taken from ground level. Photographer Keast Burke, in an article for the March 1932 *Australasian Photo-Review* entitled 'Sydney Harbour Bridge Pictures: snapshots anyone can make without a permit' encouraged amateurs to take close-ups of the steel bearings and 'aeroplane views'.

Once opened, feature filmmakers showed much more interest in using the Bridge, often to mark a passage of time for a central character. In Ken Hall's *Squatter's Daughter* (1933) the old owner

∧ When a British graphic designer came to produce a cover for the 1960 edition of *Come in Spinner*, the Bridge served to indicate the book's setting in Sydney. Pan Books, London, first published 1951

< Pokerwork stationery box, c 1933. Spearritt collection

The Little Pottery, c 1964

> Pokerwork jewelry box, c.1932. Spearritt collection.

> Cazneaux's photograph *A Minor Quay*, showing the eastern face of Bridge, with the pedestrian walkway still under construction. *The Second Bridge Book*, 1931. National Library of Australia, courtesy Cazneaux family

of Waratah Station, coming home from two years in England, tells a business associate on board ship as they near Circular Quay 'When I left here two years ago, Cartwright, I never thought I'd see that Bridge finished.' In Miles Mander's *The Flying Doctor* (1936) one of the protagonists gets work as a painter on the Bridge. In Ken Hall's *The Broken Melody* (1938) a painted backdrop of the Bridge is used for some scenes, including a failed suicide attempt. The Bridge reappears later in the film, like a rainbow. In the enormously popular *Dad and Dave Come to Town*, also released by Ken Hall in 1938, the Bridge is used as a cinematic symbol of modernity in an Australia less and less reliant on the sheep's back.

Poster artists concentrated on the form and the setting of the Bridge. Melbourne artist Percy Trompf, already well known for his Bondi beach girl poster, used an almost completed Bridge, the pylons still to rise above deck, with the slogan 'Still Building Australia'. Trompf painted the Dorman Long workshops in the foreground and the city in the background. When Douglas Annand produced his 'Sydney Bridge Celebrations' poster for the opening he had a tall, bronzed lifesaver pointing towards a pristine Bridge. James Northfield chose

a bird's eye view from the west, looking down over the Bridge, for his 1938 'Sydney Harbour' poster commissioned by the Australian National Travel Association, publishers of the magazine *Walkabout*. The British poster artist, Tom Purvis, produced a bold male head with beckoning finger to attempt to lure Britons to the Sesqui-centennial celebrations in Sydney in 1938. This strong, modern image, was in stark contrast to the much more traditional poster produced by FH Coventry, which depicted Captain Arthur Phillip overlooking his troops, the imperial flag and a handful of Aborigines, with the Bridge centre stage in the middle ground, lit up by fireworks.

When the Sydney City Council published its *Soul of the City* (1937) a lavish volume of photographs by Max Dupain, a young Sydney photographer, the city was portrayed as a living organism, and its great structures – such as the Bridge – were seen to be part of that life. The book opened with photographs

of dawn over Sydney Harbour, the Bridge in the middle distance:

> As the first glow of morning tips the Harbour shores, the great metropolis of Sydney begins to stir … Comes the army of sweepers to cleanse the City streets for the day ahead … the gardener's wagon, bursting with legumes and fruit, toiling along the highways since the small hours, reaches the Markets, where the earliest comers secure the finest products of Australian soil … the timetables of ferry service, the railways, the tramways, and the airways begin to function … the suburbs disgorge the thousands of cogs who drop into their places to set in motion the mighty machinery of the second greatest City of the British Empire.

A little later in the book, alongside photos of Mascot airport and Central Railway, is a shot of traffic on the Bridge. 'Hundreds of cars, buses and trams cross the mighty span that leads to another day of work.' This photographic image of the Bridge as a commuter bridge became the dominant depiction in the 1960s and 1970s, taken up by cartoonists when caricaturing traffic jams or public transport strikes. Dupain's *Soul of the City* closes with photographs of the swish of car headlights on the Bridge and the city centre at night from the Bridge.

'Sydney, in its star-studded mantle of light, appears as a veritable fairyland beckoning to all suburbia to come and be entertained.' The final photograph is of the Bridge deserted in the early hours of the morning.

The Bridge features prominently in the works of another still photographer, Frank Hurley, who in his *Sydney: A Camera Study*, first published in 1948, included a special section on the Bridge with captions like 'Sunbeams and steel'. Hurley also made the film *Symphony in Steel*, but like most films on the Bridge, especially those made of the construction in the late 1920s and early 1930s, the subject dwarfed the conception, producing a rather uninspired documentary style.

In the late 1930s those painters who used the Bridge in their work did not make it, as Cossington Smith, Wakelin and Black had done, the sole focus in a particular painting. In John D Moore's *Sydney Harbour* (1936) the Bridge is but one aspect of Sydney's landscape as seen from the eastern suburbs, part of the view from an apartment balcony. Moore, a Sydney born architect then in his mid-30s, was reacting against the sunny 'blue and gold' tradition of the late 19th century painters Streeton and Roberts. As art historian Sandra McGrath points out,

There are few dancing lights on the water and little bustling activity. Moore shows the viewer a dullish day with wintry clouds overhanging the leaden waters of the harbour and city. There is a classical sense of stillness which is reinforced by the strong composition of the vertical and horizontal elements in the foreground.

In Desiderius Orban's *Vanished View* (1948), painted near the site of his studio at the Rocks, the Bridge is almost back at the centre stage. Sandra McGrath writes that the painting shows the Harbour Bridge, George Street, the Quay crowded with boats, and

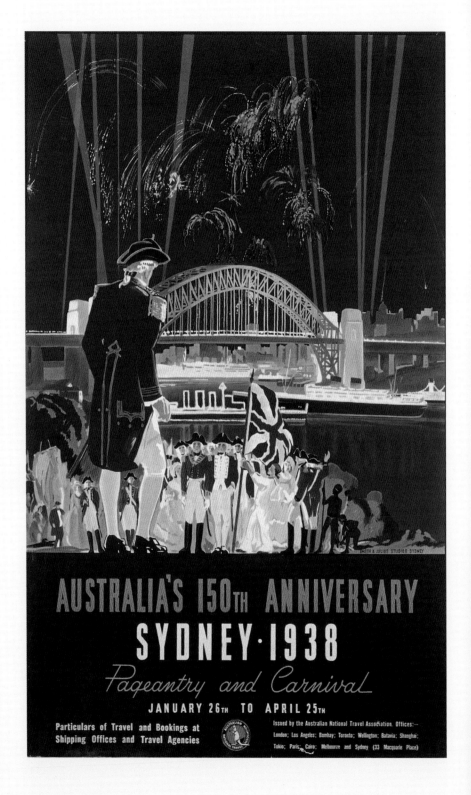

142

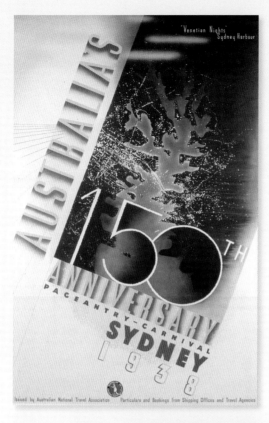

< The poster artist FH Coventry chose to portray Captain Arthur Phillip and the Sydney Harbour Bridge as his way of commemorating 150 years of European settlement, with British troops accompanied by shadowy Aboriginal figures. Australian National Travel Association 1938, Spearritt collection

> Front cover of an Australian National Travel Association brochure, with a Douglas Annand illustration of the harbour from the air at night, below a more traditional image of Sydney as the site of a Venetian carnival. Spearritt collection

the picturesque towers and dilapidated buildings of the old city. The artist has masterfully organized all these complex forms into two dynamic curves – the road and the bridge – which complements each other, while the bows of the boats create minor motifs. The striking verticals of the telegraph poles are echoed in the stanchions of the bridge and in the funnels and factory towers. Orban, unlike many other artists, sees the harbour as intimately connected with the city …

< Studio Anna vase, c 1960 Spearritt collection

∧ The British poster artist, Tom Purvis offered a strong finger of welcome, an advertisement aimed at the British market. Spearritt collection

143

^ David Moore photograph of
The Rocks from Harrington
Street in 1960. The Rocks,
owned by the state government,
remained run-down until the
opening of the Argyle Arts
Centre in an old bond building
in the late 1960s

^v Thousands of women
produced doiley images of the
Harbour Bridge, usually with
either its name or dates as part
of the decoration. They are now
prized collectors' items. Spearritt
collection, Museum of Sydney

> The Bridge and
Seidler's Blues Point
Tower apartment block
at McMahons Point.
Photograph by John Storey
from Balls Head, 2006

From siege to celebration

Artists who grew up in Sydney in the 1950s and 1960s saw grand urban development at close hand. Many of the city's sandstone buildings were destroyed to be replaced by modern skyscrapers. With the introduction of the *Strata Title Act* in 1961, which made it easier for investors or owners to purchase individual apartments, developers ran amuck with high rise apartment blocks at Kirribilli, Neutral Bay, Elizabeth Bay and further east. Many of the old harbourside homes gave way to a new-found preoccupation with having a view of the Bridge. In the 1930s you bought a block of land and used the Bridge to get to the city. In the 1960s and early 1970s boom more and more people saw themselves buying the view: the Bridge from your own loungeroom.

The harbour took centre stage in the work of Brett Whiteley, who grew up in Northwood, a harbour-side locality just west of North Sydney. In the mid-1970s he produced a whole series of harbour paintings, many as seen from his Lavender Bay studio. The Bridge figures in some form in most of the larger Sydney paintings, sometimes as a small detail as in *The Jacaranda Tree (On Sydney Harbour)*, sometimes as a prominent background as in *Lavender Bay in the Rain*, and sometimes as the centrepiece, as in his paintings of Blues Point Tower (the Seidler-designed block of flats dominating the foreshore at McMahons Point) and the Bridge competing to dominate the landscape around them.

Other avant garde filmmakers and artists took up the Bridge. Jim Sharman's film *Shirley Thompson versus the Aliens* (1972) showed for the first time a central character moving across the Bridge, when Shirley runs to join the aliens at Luna Park, where they are ensconced. The Bridge figured prominently in the work of Peter Kingston, who with fellow Oz-cartoonist Martin Sharp became committed to the conservation of Luna Park in the late 1970s. Sharp, a brilliant poster artist, delighted in juxtaposing American and Australian popular culture, taking the Eternity signwriting of Arthur Stace to a generation who had little knowledge of Sydney's cultural history. Sharp wrote of Luna Park as 'an artwork in itself, a city state of illusion'. Living in North Sydney, Peter Kingston continues to use the Bridge, the North Sydney Pool and other local icons in his work.

Sydney born David Moore (1927–2003) became the most important photographic interpreter of the Bridge from the 1940s to the 1990s. Like Cazneaux and Dupain he was fascinated with the structure itself, but he also revelled in its setting, having a life-long fascination with Sydney harbour.

∧ It took the conceptual artist Richard Tipping many months to get the Department of Main Roads to grant permission for his 'Southern Crossing' installation, erected on the south-eastern pylon for the 50th anniversary in 1982

A painting of the Bridge by his father, John D Moore, is reproduced earlier in this chapter. In the late 1940s David Moore captured traffic on the Bridge, a theme that continued to fascinate him, photographing trains and traffic both day and night in subsequent years. In the early 1960s he captured the Bridge from the Rocks, then a very depressed area of Sydney. He is best known today for his superb aerial photographs of the Bridge where Sydney harbour appears as a glistening backdrop to the tongues of land reaching out from either shore.

> Naive artists often portray the Bridge on a variety of objects. This plywood drinks tray, painted in acrylic, was purchased in 1999. Spearritt collection

Throughout its history the Bridge has also figured prominently in amateur art and crafts. The *Women's Weekly* Symphony of Steel tray cloth competition, held in 1933, produced thousands of crocheted entries, one of which is reproduced on page 144. The Bridge, and often the Opera House as well, are inevitable topics in primary school art classes. In the 1970s the Bridge became a symbol for a revival of Sydney chauvinism of the like not seen since the 1930s. The Bridge, with its striking pylons, fitted well into the rediscovery of art deco among the middle-class avant-garde, so much that Bridge souvenirs from the 1930s had, by the early 1980s, become sought-after collectors' items. Until the 1970s these souvenirs – such as cut-glass ashtrays, Shelley Ware cups, metal broaches and scale models – were universally regarded as distasteful kitsch and many were thrown out.

When the Sydney Festival replaced the lacklustre Waratah Festival as Sydney's answer to Melbourne's Moomba and Adelaide's Arts Festival, a stylised Bridge became the logo for both advertising posters and programs. Many of Sydney's young artists, both the middle-class avant-garde and the new social realists have made representations of the Bridge an important part of their work.

The Bridge remains secure in its landscape setting. Apart from a bevy of nondescript office and apartment blocks on the western side at Milsons Point, there have been few built encroachments on the Bridge or its approaches. Town planning regulations on both sides of the harbour prevent new structures from compromising vistas of the Bridge. Generations of photographers, filmmakers and artists continue to have an unimpeded view from many a vantage point.

The Opera House sits noticeably but discretely in this landscape, its sail-like shells as much a part of the harbour as the yachts. Despite its striking appearance the construction of the Opera House did not excite artists or the public to anywhere near the extent that the Bridge did. What could be more exciting than two half-arches reaching out across the harbour? To the Railway Commissioners they carried a promise of more travellers and more revenue, to the artists of the time they were a steel symphony needing just a little orchestration. Photographers, painters and filmmakers have been doing that ever since.

> A group of Bridge climbers, on their downward climb from the top of the Bridge. John Storey, 2006

Australia's icon

*The great steel structures of the last decades
of the 19th century captured the popular imagination,
with the Statue of Liberty and the Eiffel Tower
taking on symbolic as well as technological meaning. Both
structures were in great centres of urban civilisation, one
from the old world, one from the new. And in each case the
landscape setting gave them a commanding presence, which
they retain to this day. When it was first built the Eiffel
Tower overlooked formal parks and a city where few buildings
were more than six storeys high. The Statue of Liberty
commanded an entire waterway.*

< Australian National Travel Association brochure. When the Australian National Travel Association marketed Australia in the United States in the late 1930s it chose an image that included the bridge to represent the nation as 'Crossroads of the South Seas'. Spearritt collection

148

With the coming of the skyscraper, first to Chicago and New York, and later to other cities, urban structures faced much more competition. In the late 19th century some churches wanted skyscrapers banned, rejecting secular attempts to get nearer to heaven. Landmark buildings now not only had to be distinctive but had to have a landscape setting where they could be seen from near and far.

The Empire State Building, constructed in just 14 months between March 1930 and May 1931, rose 103 floors above the Manhattan skyline, the tallest building in the world at that time. Continuing the 1880s New York tradition, where new skyscrapers had an upper floor open to the public, the Empire State's purpose-built observation deck set out to be a tourist destination in its own right, and remains so to this day. Q1 on the Gold Coast, the world's tallest residential tower, opened in 2005, has an observation deck straight out of New York.

> Ceramic magnet of Sydney skyline, c 1990. Spearritt collection, Museum of Sydney

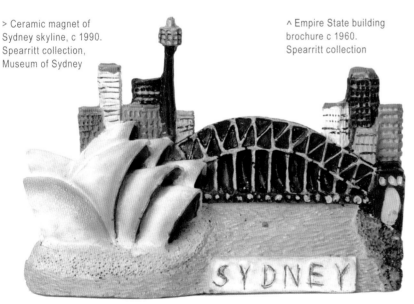

^ Empire State building brochure c 1960. Spearritt collection

There is one structure that is almost guaranteed to retain its landscape setting, a bridge. Being built over ravines or water, bridges rarely face competing structures. When planning the Harbour Bridge, Bradfield had countless great bridges to contemplate, secure in their landscapes. His ambitions for the Harbour Bridge certainly encompassed the Bridge as a destination in its own right, hence the stairways for public access in the pylons. Each pylon could be climbed, like climbing up the dome of a great cathedral. Unlike bridge designers in New York or London, Bradfield had no other notable bridges to contend with. Sydney only had a handful of bridges, from the decrepit Gladesville Bridge (1881) to the more elegant, but low slung Pyrmont Bridge (1902) (with its electrically powered swing span Pyrmont was one of the many bridges that Bradfield worked on in the late 1890s and early 1900s). Neither of these bridges carried both rail and vehicular traffic, nor did bridges elsewhere in Australia, so the Harbour Bridge dwarfed them all in both concept and execution.

With the lifting of height limits in Australian cities from the late 1950s, modern skyscrapers jostled with each other for attention, and often effectively belittled once iconic structures. Brisbane used to market itself with posters and photographs of its City Hall, a grand 1930 edifice, celebrating Brisbane as the only Australian capital city to have a metropolitan-wide council. But vistas to and from City Hall have been obliterated by office blocks. Had City Hall been on the river it might have retained some dignity.

Ancient and modern wonders

Until the 1950s most school children could have named the seven wonders of the ancient world, and those with an engineering bent might even have been able to name the seven wonders of the modern world, a much more contested list. The Sydney Harbour Bridge commonly made it into British lists in the 1930s, which included the *Queen Mary*, the Battersea Power Station and the Empire State Building, but never made it into American lists. The deliberately longer Bayonne Bridge (1931), between Staten Island and New Jersey, put a stop to that.

There have been no catastrophic accidents to mar the Bridge's reputation, as happened with the collapse of one span of the Westgate Bridge in Melbourne in October 1970. Construction deaths on the Sydney Bridge were due to inadequate safety provisions rather than faulty design. Nor has the Bridge ever suffered damage from an external source, as did Hobart's Tasman Bridge which collapsed when a central pier was rammed by a boat in 1975.

The Bridge proved to Australians that they too could become a great industrial society, as the United Kingdom, western Europe and the United States before them. Built at a time when Australia relied heavily on primary exports, it was evidence of our growing technological prowess. Seen in this light, it is easier to understand the excitement and amazement with which Australians greeted the construction of the Bridge.

Although not the longest arch bridge in the world, it remains the widest and heaviest; hence the proud and oft-repeated claim that it is the largest arch bridge in the world. Apart from the Bayonne (504 metres) there are two other steel arch bridges now longer than the Sydney Harbour Bridge, the New River Gorge Bridge (Fayetteville, USA, 1977, 518 metres in length, deck width 23 metres) and the Lupu in Shanghai (2003, 550 metres in length, deck width 29 metres). With a deck width of 49 metres, providing eight lanes of traffic, two railway tracks, and two pedestrian walkways, the Sydney Harbour Bridge remains an unusual and spectacular structure. While it has National Trust listing, and the current custodian, the RTA has a conservation management plan, it is yet to be registered as a key item of Australia's national heritage.

< Harbour Bridge in shape of a kangaroo, plaster decoration in the tradition of flying ducks to be affixed to a wall. Spearritt collection, Museum of Sydney

∨ Empire State Building brochure c 1960

The Wonders of the World —

TEMPLE OF DIANA AT EPHESUS.

PYRAMIDS OF EGYPT.

TOMB OF MAUSOLUS.

COLOSSUS OF RHODES.

8 in all—date back thousands of years. Of the ancient 7 all except the Pyramids have long since disappeared. Only 1 of the 8—New York City's fabulous Empire State Building—was built in the 20th Century. The 102-story, 1,472-foot high Empire State, now indisputably the World's No. 1 tourist attraction, is considered by many historians to be THE GREATEST WONDER OF THEM ALL!

HANGING GARDENS OF BABYLON.

PHAROS OF ALEXANDRIA.

STATUE OF ZEUS AT OLYMPIA.

'More impressive than the Eiffel Tower'

When the Pylon Lookout first opened in the southeast pylon in 1934, its proprietors asked in their *Sydney Harbour Bridge Times* broadsheet:

> Why go TO PARIS (for the Eiffel Tower)
> TO NEW YORK (for the Empire State Building)
> TO LONDON (for the Tower)
> It costs a small fortune.

A visit to the Sydney Harbour Bridge Pylon costs only ONE SHILLING and world travellers will tell you that 'Looking Down on Sydney from the top of the Harbour Bridge' is by far the greatest thrill of all of them.

To proclaim that Sydney and therefore Australia had something that the rest of the world did not was a combination of justified pride and small-town chauvinism. In the 1930s relatively few Australians could afford to travel overseas. It took at least a month by boat to get to Europe. For many, particularly those from country areas and other

^ Hand painted Studio Anna vase. Spearritt collection

< *Pylon Lookout* brochure, 14th edition, 1962. Although the pylons were steam-cleaned in 1961, the Pylon Lookout didn't always update its cover photo, showing the pylons covered in the grime of Sydney as a working port

^ The advertisement is from *Gregory's Guide to Sydney* c 1950. Spearritt collection

States, the Bridge was the only modern wonder of the world they were ever likely to see.

The Pylon Lookout soon became one of Sydney's major tourist attractions, for both Sydneysiders and out-of-town visitors. Not content with telescopes, the proprietors added penny peep-shoes, distorting mirrors, model railways and a rooster with a 5.5-metre tail. Although the Lookout had to compete with nearby Luna Park from 1935 (built on the site of the Dorman Long workshops), it still managed to attract 500 000 people between 1934 and 1942, when it was closed to make way for anti-aircraft guns, placed on top of all four pylons.

∧ Ezy-Bilt catalogue front cover, from Ezy-Bilt, a South Australian manufacturer of metal toy models, Australia's answer to the British Meccano firm. Griffin Press, Adelaide c 1955

LOOK INSIDE THE PYLON !

KEY TO EXHIBITS
PYLON LOOKOUT, SYDNEY HARBOUR BRIDGE

The rough concrete structures which housed the guns are still visible today.

The Lookout reopened in 1949, with a new proprietor, Melbourne-born Yvonne Rentoul, who settled in Sydney after the war. She rapidly accumulated an all-Australian exhibition, including dioramas of 'our historical background, primary and secondary industries and love of sport'. Other dioramas included banking, secondary industries, defence and transport. Many more attractions were to be found in the body of the pylon, but the principal attraction was the rooftop, with its 'five million acre view' from the Blue Mountains to the Tasman Sea. As if those, 'giant electric binoculars' and a broadcast description in three languages were not enough, there were the 'famous white cats' with their colourful merry-go-round and wishing well. The cats, designed to appeal to children, were featured on a variety of souvenirs.

< This cross-section of the Pylon Lookout shows the narrow stair access from the roadway level (one way up, another down, exactly the same as it is today) and then the more elaborate stair access to the main exhibits. Pylon Lookout 1962

> *Pylon Lookout Souvenir* postal booklet. This souvenir, produced in the 1950s, reminded visitors of the many ways that they could view Sydney from the Pylon Lookout, the city's premier viewing point. Spearritt collection

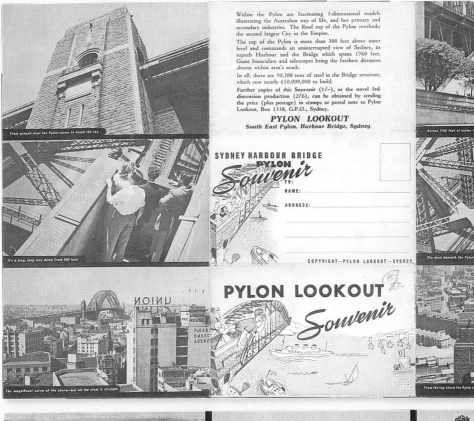

Within the Pylon are fascinating 3-dimensional models illustrating the Australian way of life, and her primary and secondary industries. The Roof top of the Pylon overlooks the second largest City in the Empire.

The top of the Pylon is more than 300 feet above water level and commands an uninterrupted view of Sydney, its superb Harbour and the Bridge which spans 1760 feet. Giant binoculars and telescopes bring the farthest distances almost within arm's reach.

In all, there are 50,300 tons of steel in the Bridge structure, which cost nearly £10,000,000 to build.

Further copies of this Souvenir (1/–), or the novel 3rd-dimension production (2/6), can be obtained by sending the price (plus postage) in stamps or postal note to Pylon Lookout, Box 1338, G.P.O., Sydney.

PYLON LOOKOUT
South East Pylon, Harbour Bridge, Sydney.

SYDNEY HARBOUR BRIDGE
PYLON
Souvenir
TO:
NAME:
ADDRESS:

COPYRIGHT—PYLON LOOKOUT—SYDNEY.

PYLON LOOKOUT *Souvenir*

From ground level the Pylon seems to touch the sky.

It's a long, long way down from 300 feet.

The magnificent curve of the chord—but not all the steel is straight.

Across 1760 feet of water the great Bridge stands, its feet secure on the Pylons.

The deck beneath the Pylon is wide enough for four train lines and six streams of cars.

From the top chord the Pylon stands up against the sky.

^ The author inspecting the Bridge from the Pylon Lookout, now operated by Bridge Climb, in September 2006. Photograph by John Storey

The Bridge and Pylon tower above the City.

Miller's Point—and its shipping activity are beneath the Pylon.

The Japanese Naval Binoculars show some surprising sights.

Even the biggest Overseas vessels can pass beneath the Bridge.

Write your letter here.

Little ferry boats chuff under the steel lacework of the Bridge.

The maze of the City is bewildering.

The graceful arch from which the roadway is suspended.

Circular Quay is the front door to Sydney.

This postcard, from late 1931, expressed a common view among visiting Melburnians

< Taken on 1 October 1931, this photograph shows the finishing touches being put on the south-eastern pylon. The Bridge towered over Circular Quay and the convict-built sandstone bondstores in the Rocks. State Records New South Wales NRS12685

decision to close it in 1971, though at the time they pleaded lack of office space. Mrs Rentoul fought a valiant battle but lost. Certainly the Lookout had been a highly commercial – some would say vulgar – operation, but it had also been popular. Until 1962, when the observation deck on the 25-storey AMP Building at the Quay opened, the Lookout had a monopoly of tourists seeking an aerial view of Sydney. Only a select few were allowed up the 111-metre AWA Tower in York Street (which was opened in 1939). The Pylon Lookout's monopoly was further eroded in 1967, with the opening of the 50-storey Australia Square Tower. Its enclosed viewing deck soon put the AMP out of business and made the Pylon Lookout seem old hat. The Seidler-designed tower became the first structure in Sydney, at 171 metres, to be higher than the Bridge (the top of the arch is 134 metres above sea level).

On eviction in 1971 Mrs Rentoul said that even though she had to go she did not want to see the pylon closed. It was closed – amid scant protest – and used by the DMR to store various relics associated with the building of the Bridge. The up surge of interest in Sydney's history in the late 1970s, encouraged by the Wran Labor government, local historians and the universities, saw the Pylon Lookout reopened in 1982 under government auspices, incorporating some of the objects and displays which existed in Bradfield's museum, briefly open to the public in the 1930s in the southwest pylon.

Tooth's bitter ale label, c 1935. Spearritt collection

The Pylon Lookout became Australia's greatest tourist trap, its atmosphere similar to the tourist shops surrounding the Leaning Tower of Pisa or St Peter's Basilica, though Mrs Rentoul did manage to keep her pylon remarkably free of carved names and initials. Embarrassment about the high level of commercialisation and the tattiness of some of the exhibits was probably the real reason for the DMR's

Sydney's coathanger, Australia's icon

On completion, the Bridge became the unrivalled symbol of Australia overseas for at least four decades and even now it is probably more widely photographed and just as readily recognised as its only competitor, the Sydney Opera House, opened in 1973. Why does Australia present a bridge as its symbol? The United States has its Statue of Liberty, Britain its Houses of Parliament, and Russia the Kremlin. The Bridge has none of the overt political overtones associated with these structures and is more akin in its symbolic quality to the Eiffel Tower or the Statue of Liberty, both immense physical and technological achievements in their day. The Bridge can perhaps be seen as an embodiment of the alleged petit bourgeois aspirations of the Australian 'masses' who would prefer the surety of concrete and steel to a symbol based on ideas or ideals.

The Bridge's dominance has grown rather than diminished with Sydney's growth. It once presided over a down-at-heel Circular Quay and the Bridge itself was equally down at heel. Postcards in the 1950s show brown pylons, filthy with urban grime and pollution. Regular steam cleaning only began in 1961. With the building boom of the late 1950s and early 1960s the Quay became a showcase for the office blocks of modern Australian and international capitalism. The development of the twin city of North Sydney in the 1960s and early 1970s emphasised again that the Bridge links two halves of a great city. The painter Lloyd Rees saw the growth of skyscrapers in North Sydney as bringing symmetry back to a lopsided landscape. From many vantage points today the tower blocks of Sydney and North Sydney appear as natural adjuncts to the pylons.

Becoming Australia's symbol was not achieved without a fight. The press in other States were quick to point out that the Bridge belonged to Sydney and not them. Two days after the opening the Hobart *Mercury* observed that the Bridge 'is not a national work, except in that Australian material

∧ The 1953 cover of the *Australian Junior Encyclopedia* attempted to sum up, graphically, the Australian experience

< Coathanger bridge in coathanger wire, c 1982. Spearritt collection, Museum of Sydney

THE AUSTRALIAN JUNIOR ENCYCLOPÆDIA

THE AUSTRALIAN JUNIOR ENCYCLO-PÆDIA VOL. II.

156

^ The photo-montage cover of the *AM* magazine was published the day before the Queen became the first reigning monarch to set foot on Australian soil. Accompanied by Prince Philip, she is welcomed to Sydney by Prime Minister Menzies

< The July 1949 cover of the British magazine *Autocar* featured the Austin, a product of British engineering, like the Bridge. But the American firm General Motors had already won federal government approval to build Australia's first car, the Holden, which came off the assembly line in November 1948

was used'. Adelaide's St Peter's College magazine had a clearer notion of the likely symbolic importance of the Bridge: 'we are doing our share with the other states of the Commonwealth in paying for Sydney's monumental structure, even though we may never have the opportunity of setting foot upon it'. Although the Melbourne press often made fun of the Bridge, Melburnians themselves flocked to the opening in their thousands. Eight special trains left Spencer Street Station on 16 and 17 March carrying 3500 Victorian visitors to the opening. Despite their numbers the Victorians were granted no place at the official opening, which may be one reason why the Melbourne-based *Australasian* commented caustically at the opening 'the people of Sydney could not afford the Bridge. It will be a financial burden all their lives.' The *Argus* was even more explicit: 'Sydney … wants to walk across the bridge before the Commonwealth puts in the bailiffs and has the thing removed.'

The Sydney press tackled Melbourne's churlishness head on. *Smith's Weekly*, with its trademark racism, saw the Bridge as the ultimate victory of Sydney over Melbourne:

> Melbourne can no longer say to Sydney that in the making of a seaport we did little that blackfellows could not have done. Over this their Harbour, their beautiful Harbour, their unexcelled Harbour, the Sydneyites have thrown the biggest, solidest, heaviest bridge ever constructed by the hand of man [19 March 1932].

Premier Lang did his best in his opening speech to stress the national and international importance of the Bridge. This left-wing firebrand, hated by conservatives, called on the rhetoric of Empire when summing up his feelings about the Bridge:

157

Australia! So vast, varied, so filled with the unexpected and unusual . . . that time alone can tell her story! Give time a chance, therefore, and plan at least a month's visit . . . your return, a lifetime of memories! Partly because Nature is so unbelievable in its weird survivals . . . partly because, in a brief time, man has built a new and energetic nation, you'll like Australia! And you'll be surprised by her sweeping beauty and ideal climate (her seasons are reversed) . . . her vivid sports and infectious, happy welcome!

No other voyage compares with your approach to this continent of contrasts. A romantic South Pacific Cruise, with stops at Hawaii, Samoa, Fiji, New Zealand. Expenses moderate . . . the exchange always favorable.

150TH BIRTHDAY CELEBRATIONS
Jan. 26 to Apr. 25, 1938, at Sydney

A century and a half of peaceful progress! Marked by historic and military pageants; the British Empire Games; the Royal Easter Show; by sports, exhibits, gaiety . . . in the midst of the Summer season! Her million-peopled cities will be gayer than ever before; her friendly, prosperous, English-speaking people in the mood to welcome visitors.

Australia

Complete details and literature obtainable from Travel Agents or:

AUSTRALIAN NATIONAL TRAVEL ASSOCIATION
[A non-profit Community Organization]
Suite 318 B, Hotel Clark, Los Angeles, California

Identification
National Magazines
Country Life—November, 1937
Harpers Bazaar—January, 1938
Vogue—November, 1937
House & Garden—November, 1937

Advertisement No. 11-2-1
One-half Page

Final Proof

Australian National Travel Association

Bowman, Deute, Cummings, Inc.

<vThese two koda-chrome slides, taken in 1979, show Sydney at a time when the Rocks was still run-down and the coal-fired electric power stations were still belching smoke in and near the metropolis. The Rocks is being redeveloped, while the smoke stacks are a reminder of just how dirty parts of Sydney were when industry still dominated much of the waterfront to the west of the Bridge.
Photographs Jill Abbott

< Marketing Australia to the American market, making reassuring comments about the trip by liner to Australia, with a friendly koala welcome and the Bridge as an indication of civilisation.
Australian National Travel Association 1938

^ Pewter bottle stopper, c 1990. Ingenuity in Bridge souvenirs became more common during and after the 50th anniversary celebrations in 1982.
Spearritt collection, Museum of Sydney

The engineering brains and the financial facilities of the centre of the Empire have combined with the skill, the labour and determination of the Australian people … It is an adornment to the city to which it belongs, and above that, is a pride to the whole Empire.

In Britain the *Sheffield Daily Telegraph* called it the 'World's Greatest Bridge' while *The Newcastle Journal* stressed that it had been made 'largely from Yorkshire material'. The American *Time* magazine had a less charitable interpretation of what the Bridge meant, but it nonetheless remarked on and photographed it, launching its international career as Australia's symbol.

Into Sydney's dream bridge New South Wales has flung $50 000 000 … Unquestionably Australia, free and easy as a cowboy on payday, has 'flung' millions which could have been saved into her Sydney Harbour Bridge. Her Labor Government insisted on paying the bridge workmen on a sliding scale which slid as living prices soared in Sydney. Originally the bridge was estimated to cost only $10 000 000.

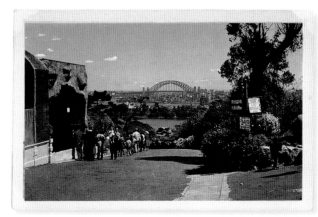

< The Bridge can be seen from many vantage points around Sydney. One of the best known vistas is from Taronga Zoo, Australia's most popular zoo, with a magnificent site at Mosman, commanding views of the harbour. Postcard c 1960

OPENING OF
SYDNEY HARBOUR BRIDGE
19TH MARCH 1932

> This framed photograph by Hall of the opening of the Bridge took pride of place in the author's flat in Hayes Street, Neutral Bay, above a rosewood leadlight cabinet housing the author's Harbour Bridge collection. Photograph by John Storey 1981. Items on display now in the Spearritt collection, Museum of Sydney

150ᵗʰ ANNIVERSARY OF AUSTRALIA —— 1788–1938

From symbol to brand

The battle for Australia's symbol, first fought out in tourist brochures and reference books, continues on websites and in all forms of tourist promotion. A brief perusal of brochures and reference books published between the 1930s and the 1980s shows that the Bridge was invariably used as an opening picture, usually with a caption along the lines of 'gateway to Australia'. And Sydney was indeed the gateway to Australia. Before jet air travel, almost all overseas visitors to Australia came by ship. Their first port of call (especially from Britain) was usually Fremantle, but many did not disembark till Sydney, at wharves near the Bridge. As soon as you entered the harbour you could see the arch in the distance; you knew you had arrived in Sydney.

The Bridge has been so clearly dominant in Sydney for the last 80 years that until the coming of the Opera House it had no rivals as the symbol for the capital of New South Wales. The choice of symbols for other State capitals has always been less clear-cut. Melbourne used to oscillate between parks and churches, with an occasional late

afternoon shot of the notoriously brown Yarra River. The Victorian government occasionally sets up a committee to provide Melbourne with a spectacular landmark, but has had to be content with some of Australia's tallest skyscrapers, the Rialto (1986, 251 metres) and the Eureka Tower (2005, 297 metres), trumped while it was being built by the Q1 skyscraper on the Gold Coast, at 323 metres, with its striking spire.

Adelaide managed to replace its parks and churches with its Festival Theatre, but that's now old hat. Brisbane and Perth go for shots of apartment and office towers, as if to prove that Sydney and Melbourne are not the only Australian cities with skyscrapers. Hobart, sensibly, never bothered to try, content to market the intimacy of Salamanca Place.

Canberra's Parliament House (1988) is built into the side of a hill. It has lavish public rooms and interiors, and well-marketed flagpole. The cultural and judicial structures on Lake Burley Griffin cancel each other out. The Black Mountain Telecommunications Tower in Canberra

ㄴ Coffee set, made by Halltonware in England, c 1935. Spearritt collection

With a rec
Her Maje...

160

< Sesquicentennial letterhead designers had no difficulty in finding a symbol for Sydney, even recognising prior Aboriginal occupation, but the other capital cities were much less distinct

∧ Ansett airlines, in this ad in the Melbourne *Age*, 8 April 1981, used the Bridge as a powerful negative symbol, indicating that they flew direct from Melbourne to Brisbane

> In this handkerchief, manufactured in the late 1970s, Sydney bristles with iconic structures. The Bridge, at 139 metres, remained the tallest structure in the City, until the Australia Square Tower, at 170 metres, opened in 1967. Spearritt collection

< The *Australian Women's Weekly* prepared its two million readers for the coming of the SS *Gothic*, carrying HM *Queen Elizabeth II*, through Sydney Heads. Here a koala atop the Bridge has the British flag in one hand and the Blue Ensign in the other, for a 'real Aussie welcome'

1954	February					1954
Sun.	Mon.	Tues.	Wed.	Thur.	Fri.	Sat.
	1	2	3	4	5	6
7	8	9	10	11	12	13
14	15	16	17	18	19	20
21	22	23	24	25	26	27
28						

ussie" welcome for

Queen Elizabeth II arrives Sydney, Feb. 3rd.

has many similarities with the Sydney Tower (1981, formerly Centrepoint) including the temptation that builders of such structures have to install a revolving restaurant, often serving indifferent food. Neither of these structures is in any way exceptional. Equivalent observation towers can be found in every continent.

The Bridge continues to generate more souvenirs than any other structure or building in Australia, its only competitor the Opera House, with a similar grand setting and an equally distinctive shape. The range of souvenirs is certainly as extensive as the kitsch associated with the Eiffel Tower, the British royal family, the Empire State Building or the Leaning Tower of Pisa. The Bridge also generates replica models by many a

161

Australia Day, 1988, saw Circular Quay and the Bridge centre stage, as crowds filled the harbour and surrounds for the Tall Ships. Kodachrome transparencies, Peter Spearritt, 1988

< Velvet cushion covers featuring the Bridge were popular from the 1930s to the 1980s. Spearritt collection

MOLNAR
24. 8. 66

Good idea, but we must think of the future ... What shall we put on top of the restaurant?

^ When the architect George Molnar drew this cartoon for the *Sydney Morning Herald* in August 1966 Sydney had recently seen the opening of a restaurant on top of Seidler's Australia Square Tower

remember, are the exact figures, or near enough to give an impression of its size, which increases rapidly as you approach it. It has been called a Titan's coat-hanger, a circumflex accent over the song of a metropolis, and even likened by the poet Hugh McCrae to his mistress's eyebrow.

By the late 1950s the Bridge had become a universal symbol of Australia in feature films, especially those which hoped to get an overseas audience. It appeared in *The Summer of the 17th Doll* (1959), even though the original play was set in Melbourne, and in *They're a Weird Mob* (1968). It appeared in over 20 feature films made in the 1970s, including the opening sequences in *The Adventures of Barry Mackenzie* (1972), and as many again in the 1980s including *Heatwave* and *Star Struck* (1982). In recent years it has starred in *Mad Max Beyond Thunderdome* (1985) and *Mission Impossible 2* (2000), along with *Finding Nemo* (2003).

would-be civil engineer. Replica models have been made out of many materials. A number of houses in Sydney suburbs once had – a few still do – gateposts topped by a miniature Bridge in steel. Matches were a popular replica-building material; the Pylon Lookout proudly displayed a model Bridge made out of 200 000 of them!

Like similar structures the world over, Sydney's Bridge has often suffered at the hands of advertising copy writers. In 1952 the Sydney poet Kenneth Slessor – tired of the exaggerated claims and inflated detail of the tourist brochures – wrote:

> Something, I suppose, must be said about the Harbour Bridge. It elbows itself into any description of Sydney as truculently as it forces its presence on the city. The Bridge is 20 miles high, weighs 736,000 Persian yakmans (which is roughly equivalent to 24,000,000 Turkish yusdrums), is 142 miles, 17 rods, 23 poles, 5 perches in length, carries everything from rickshaws to electric buggies, and feeds on paint. These, as I think I

As the competition for tourists intensifies, both within countries and between countries, tourist symbols have become tourist brands. The Bridge has long been promoted by New South Wales and Commonwealth government authorities. In 1987 the Commonwealth government's Australian Tourist Commission, moved its headquarters from Melbourne to Sydney and the 1988 Bicentennial celebrations were directed from an office block in the Rocks. The Bridge gained renewed prominence with the announcement in 1993 that Sydney would host the 2000 Olympic Games. The Bridge and the Opera House have added substance to Tasmanian journalist Charles Whitham's 1927 claim that Circular Quay was 'the chief theatre of Australian life'. The Bridge went from symbol to brand in the late 1990s when a group of businessmen figured out that you could charge people to walk over it. This is not an option for the Opera House.

Bridge Climb

Entrepreneurs long speculated about how the Bridge could be turned into a more active tourist attraction, and how they could make money out of it. In 1957 one group planned to turn the top chord into the world's grandest scenic railway, with observation cars going over it. Mrs Rentoul wanted a cable car from the Pylon Lookout to Mrs Macquarie's Chair, like the flying fox at Niagara Falls. When Paul Cave, a Sydney tile merchant who had developed a great fondness for the Bridge, first thought about walking paying customers over it, most people thought he was mad.

The drama of walking on top of the Bridge, captured here by photographer John Storey in September 2006. The Australian flag and the New South Wales flag are both flying. The flags flown are controlled by the New South Wales government, and even local football team flags are occasionally allowed to flutter

It had always been possible to walk over the arch. Indeed, because of the labor-intensive nature of construction and subsequent maintenance, the very structure provided for people to walk over it, with a graduated stairway on the top and chord bottom. Some thousands of people did so between 1932 and the opening of Cave's Bridge Climb in 1998. Most, including this author, were guests of the DMR, and were compelled to sign an undertaking that you wouldn't sue for negligence if you fell. Others climbed illicitly, often as a prank, some more dangerously under the influence of alcohol.

The single biggest issue that faced Paul Cave and his backers was how to get people up and back safely, and how to do so in such a way that insurers would issue Bridge Climb Pty Ltd with coverage.

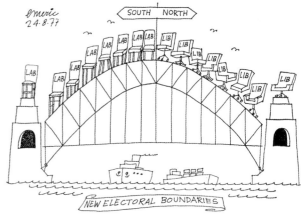

After a variety of schemes, including metal shoes that would magnetically cling to the steel, the group came up with the idea of a static line, linking climbers both to a railing and to each other in groups of ten. This makes suicide impossible and reassures nervous climbers through group solidarity.

Bridge Climb negotiated with the RTA for some years before signing a lease agreement, a proportion of their revenue going to the RTA for Bridge maintenance. Since it opened on 1 October 1998 well over 2 million people have climbed the Bridge and the price has tripled.

The first large working Bridge in the world to have a commercial climbing operation has given Bridge Climb a phenomenal amount of free publicity, both in Australia and overseas. The Sydney Harbour Bridge currently gets 1 million hits on Google, with Bridge Climb coming out first. Every tourist guide and website mentions it, to the extent that some overseas tourists do not realise that you can walk across the pedestrian pathway or use the cycle way, abutting the roadway on either side of the Bridge, for nothing. Bridge Climb also runs the Pylon Lookout and is contractually obliged to develop a substantial museum about the Bridge. To this end, Paul Cave outbid public museums in Sydney to secure de Groot's sword.

Whose bridge?

Some dismiss the Bridge as technologically passé, aesthetically repulsive, or inadequate for the traffic it is expected to carry. In 1951 the American writer James Michener wrote that 'the symbol of Australia' was big, utilitarian and ugly. Nonetheless its sheer physical presence has the same majesty now as it did in the interwar years. Recent developments, including the demolition of the Water Police wharves and their replacement with the Hyatt

Hotel in 1989, have preserved the landscape setting. Pedestrians and cyclists are catered for with a dignity that is hard to find elsewhere in central Sydney. In our current era of low-maintenance concrete bridges, it is a labour-intensive structure, providing employment for maintenance workers, traffic controllers, tow truck drivers, security guards, Bridge Climb's tour guides and toll collectors, who collected their last tolls in January 2009, made redundant by electronic tolling.

Was the Christian Socialist, the Reverend A Rivett, exaggerating when he wrote this for the AWU's *Worker* at the opening?

> Here is a structure that is altruistic from beginning to end. It is a consummate piece of socialism – yea more, of pure Communalism. The Bridge exists for all. The pauper and the peer will jostle side by side as they step out … Let the people of Sydney get the right angle which is: prospective of a future when the many barriers, artificial, antisocial and antichristian that now divide men, classes and nations shall disappear. The Bridge is nothing less than a sacrificial offering laid upon the altar of manhood, womanhood and childhood, and should inspire many a helpful message from the prophets in the pulpits to the people in the pews on Sunday next.

< A Bridge Climb group on the top chord, photographed by John Storey from the Pylon Lookout in September 2006. For safety reasons, Bridge Climb does not allow climbers to carry mobile phones, cameras or other such items, but does offer a photographic memento to climbers

∧ Eternity, 1999 New Years Eve. Courtesy City of Sydney and First Light Photography

> In reflecting on the new millennium the *Sydney Morning Herald's* Alan Moir drew on a rich cartooning tradition, emphasising the longevity of Aboriginal occupation of Australia

CELEBRATING OUR 43RD MILLENNIUM..

167

< New Year's Eve fireworks, now placed on the bridge itself rather than on barges nearby, allowed quintessential Melbourne cartoonist Michael Leunig the opportunity to have a good dig at Sydney. *The Age*, 5 January 2008

The Revered Rivett may have been vindicated when Arthur Stace's Eternity calligraphy featured in a huge neon sign on the Bridge at the start of the new century. The fireworks at the Bridge opening in 1932 came from the shoreline and barges. Fireworks from the Bridge itself first appeared in the Bicentennial celebrations (1988) after the DMR agreed that the Bridge could be used for such a display. In 1982 it had taken months for artist Richard Tipping to get his light sculpture temporarily installed on one of the pylons.

The harbour had long been a site for fireworks displays, for special events, like royal visits and New Year's Eve. But fireworks from the Bridge proved so spectacular that they became a standard fixture of New Year's Eve with crowds gathering at hundreds of viewing points. The Bridge fireworks are now broadcast around the world, Sydney being the only Australian city to feature in the international television coverage. When the Carr Labor government gave permission to the Council for Aboriginal Reconciliation to take over the Bridge roadway for the People's Walk for Reconciliation on 28 May 2000, the symbolic power of the Bridge was plain to all. Up to 300 000 people walked on the day. Not all uses of the Bridge are so idealistic. In 2006 Premier Morris Iemma requested that the Sydney Swans' flag be flown from the top of the Bridge before the AFL Grand Final. They lost to the West Coast Eagles by one point.

The barriers that divide us have not come down. Rivett's optimism was misplaced. In the late 1930s and the early post-war years some lower paid workers could afford to buy land on the North Shore, just as the Labor Party had hoped when it supported the Bridge Bill in 1922. But since then the North Shore has become the largest site of middle-class settlement in Australia. Most of the suburbs the Bridge serves to the north of the harbour have returned conservative candidates over the last 80 years and a majority of Sydney's high income earners live in those suburbs. Nonetheless, the clientele for the Bridge, including those who walk across it or use public transport, is much less exclusively middle class than that for the Opera House. The Bridge links the two halves of Australia's most unequal city but it exists for all.

> Sydney Harbour Bridge mulga wood bookends, hand painted, manufactured by Humphries, Sydney, c 1936. Spearritt collection

When the first edition of this book came out in 1982 no one had written a book about the Bridge for some decades. The 50th anniversary celebrations saw the publication of David Ellyard and Richard Raxworthy's *The Proud Arch* and Ursula Prunster's *The Sydney Harbour Bridge 1932–1982* which drew on paintings, drawings and photographs.

More recent publications include Raxworthy's biography of JJC Bradfield, *An Unreasonable Man* (Hale & Iremonger, 1989), which draws on Raxworthy's extensive oral histories with bridge workers, as does Peter Lalor's *The Bridge* (2005), which also cites Bradfield's extant office diaries for the first time. Andrew Moore's biography *Francis de Groot* sheds light on both the New Guard and the de Groot incident. *Bridging Sydney*, edited by Caroline Mackenness, provides a detailed account of the Bridge's prehistory.

For a general introduction to New South Wales there is no better place to start that Beverley Kingston's *A History of New South Wales* (Cambridge University Press, 2006). For general Sydney context see Peter Spearritt *Sydney's Century: A History* (UNSW Press, 2000) and Ian Hoskins *Sydney Harbour: A History* (UNSW Press, 2009). The online version of the *Australian Dictionary of Biography* (<http://www.adb.online.anu.edu.au>) provides biographical information on both politicians and engineers. Details of all the Royal Commissions mentioned, along with debates in the New South Wales Parliament can be accessed from the Parliamentary website (<http://www.parliament.nsw.gov.au>).

Primary sources

This book draws on the newspapers of the time, mentioned in the text, including the *Sydney Morning Herald*, the *Daily Telegraph* and the *Sun*, as well as the Labor newspapers, the *Labor Daily* and *The World*. The *Sydney Mail*, *Smith's Weekly* and the *Bulletin* also carried a great deal of material and comment about the Bridge. All the major periodicals in Sydney focused at one time or another on the Bridge, from trade periodicals including *Building, Lighting, Engineering* to cultural productions, from *Sydney Opinion* to *Art in Australia*.

The first edition of this book drew heavily on a commemorative volume of photographs, *Erection Wages*, which the author donated to the Museum of Sydney in 2002. He retains a set of negatives of these prints. Most of these photographs can now be viewed on the State Records NSW site, Series number 12685, which has over 2500 photographs taken between 1923 and 1933, an important public resource. In 2003

the author donated much of his Harbour Bridge collection, including objects and paper-based items, to the Museum of Sydney, and these are sourced in captions in this book. Other items that remain in his personal collection are indicated simply as Spearritt collection. Unless otherwise noted, all illustrations from printed sources in this edition are from this collection.

Information about the Bayonne Bridge comes from the holdings of the New York Historical Society, including Port of New York Progress Report

Sources and further reading

on Kill Van Kull Bridge, 1930 and Metropolitan Highways New York, New Jersey, 1947. The best collection of documentary films about the Bridge is held by the National Film Archive in Canberra (<http://www.nfsa@afc.gov.au> All the early documentaries praise the bravery of the workmen, but not one mentions construction deaths. Television documentaries were also made for the 50th and 75th anniversaries, including Simon Nasht's *Constructing Australia: The Bridge* in 2007.

Interviews for the first edition of this book (1982) are listed on p. 117 of that volume. I have spoken to hundreds of people about the Bridge since then, from maintenance workers to supervising engineers, many of whom continue to send me newscuttings and other items. I had a number of discussions with Paul Cave and his colleagues in the formative stages of Bridge Climb, and met a cross-section of 'stakeholders' in the Bridge at the RTA/

Godden Mackay Logan seminar on 21 September 2006. A comprehensive guide to archival holdings on Bradfield can be found in the Raxworthy biography, which also includes an extensive list of Bradfield's publications (1989), as does the guide to Bradfield's papers held by the National Library of Australia. The websites of State Records New South Wales (the government archives) (<http://www.records.nsw.gov.au>), the State Library of New South Wales (including the Mitchell Library) (<http://www.sl.nsw.gov.au>), the National Library of Australia (<http://www.nla.gov.au>) and the Fisher Library (<http://www.library.usyd.edu.au/libraries/fisher>) at the University of Sydney can be searched online for both printed and manuscript material. Increasingly it is possible to search for photographs and plans on these websites as well.

Planning, engineering and construction

Bradfield, JJC, 'Linking Sydney with North Sydney', *Sydney University Engineering Society Journal*, 1913, pp 95–163

——— 'Report on the Proposed *Electrification of Railways* for the City of Sydney', *New South Wales Parliamentary Papers*, 1915–16

——— 'The City and Suburban Electric Railways and the Sydney Harbour Bridge', unpublished Doctor of Science thesis in engineering, University of Sydney, 1924

——— *Sydney Harbour Bridge: report on tenders*, Government Printer, Sydney, 1924, 63 pp

——— 'The City Railway' in *Electrification of Sydney and Suburban Railways*, Institute of Engineers Australia Transactions, vol VII, 1927, pp 293–372

Dorman Long, *The Sydney Harbour Bridge*, Dorman Long, Middlesborough, 1932, 90 pp

Freeman, Ralph and Ennis, Lawrence, 'Sydney Harbour Bridge: Manufacture of the Structural Steelwork and Erection of the Bridge', *Proceedings of the Institution of Civil Engineers*, vol 238, part 2, 1933–34

Photography, art and drawing

The largest single collection of photographs, from the Department of Public Works and the Railways, is held by the State Archives of New South Wales. The Mitchell Library has the largest holdings of wider Sydney material, including Sydney harbour. Moore Theological College holds the Frank Cash originals, while the Australian Centre for Photography holds some of Henri Mallard's works. Publications in the early 1930s included:

Cash, EFN, *Parables of the Sydney Harbour Bridge*, Sydney, 1930, 518 pp

Cazneaux, Harold, *The Bridge Book*, Art in Australia, Sydney, 1930, 26 pp

Cazneaux, Harold and others *The Second Bridge Book*, Ure Smith, Sydney, 1931, 24 pp

Curtis, Robert Emerson, *Building the Bridge*, Simmons, Sydney, 1933 (twelve lithographs, reprinted by Collins in 1982 with the addition of two more lithographs)

Wills, Colin and 'Wep' (Pidgeon, WE), *Rhymes of Sydney*, Sydney, 1933, 48 pp (reprinted by Pylon Press 1982, poems by Colin Wills, illustration by 'Wep')

The opening and subsequent anniversaries

Pamphlets, brochures and newspaper supplements held by Historic Houses Trust Library, Mitchell Library, National Library of Australia and in the author's collection. The following are held by major libraries:

Sydney Harbour Bridge Official Souvenir and Programme, Government Printer, Sydney, 1932, 180 pp

Sydney Harbour Bridge: 50, Redpath Dorman Long and Freeman Fox & Partners, UK, 1982, 20 pp

'Sydney Harbour Bridge 1932–1982', *Main Roads*, March 1982, vol 47, no 1, 32 pp

The Bridge Opened: illustrated supplement to the official souvenir, Government Printer, Sydney, March 1932, 36 pp (reprinted by Pylon Press, 1982. There is no mention of the de Groot incident in this official publication.)

Contemporary books and articles

Planning and construction of the Bridge, including role of Bradfield

Dance, HE, *Sydney Harbour Bridge*, Thomas Nelson, 1946, 34 pp

Ellyard, David and Raxworthy, Richard, *The Proud Arch: the story of the Sydney Harbour Bridge*, Bay Books, Sydney, 1982, 160 pp

Lalor, Peter, *The Bridge: the epic story of*

an *Australian icon*, Allen & Unwin, Sydney, 2005, 381 pp

Mackaness, Caroline (ed), *Bridging Sydney*, Historic Houses Trust, 2006, 285 pp (includes chapters on politics, Bradfield, the construction and a lavishly illustrated 170 page chronology from 1789 to 1932)

Raxworthy, Richard, *The Unreasonable Man: the life and works of JJC Bradfield*, Hale & Iremonger, Sydney, 1989, 153 pp

Spearritt, Peter, *The Sydney Harbour Bridge: a life*, 1st edition, Allen & Unwin, Sydney, 1982, 120 pp

North Sydney

Marshall, Sam, *Luna Park Just for Fun*, Luna Park Reserve Trust, Sydney, 1995, 152 pp

Park, Margaret, *Building a Bridge for Sydney: the North Sydney connection*, North Sydney Council, 2000, 29 pp

Sydney city

Fitzgerald, Shirley, *Sydney 1842–1992*, Hale & Iremonger, Sydney, 1992, 324 pp (definitive history of the Sydney City Council and the varying territory it has administered)

Moruya quarry and Granite Town

Greig, Helen, *Not Forgotten: memorials in granite*, Moruya, 1993, 96 pp

Neilson, Nigel, 'Granite Town-Moruya River: a chronicle of the almost forgotten people who quarried for the Sydney Harbour Bridge', unpublished Graduate Diploma in Local and Applied History, Armidale CAE, 1988, 69 pp

Lang and de Groot

Moore, Andrew, *Francis de Groot: Irish fascist, Australian legend*, Federation Press, Sydney, 2005, 222 pp

Nairn, Bede, *The 'Big Fella': Jack Lang and the Australian Labor Party 1891–1949*, MUP, 1986, 369 pp

Radi, Heather and Spearritt, Peter (eds), *Jack Lang*, Hale & Iremonger, Sydney, 1977, 326 pp

Planning and transport in Sydney

Ashton, Paul, *Planning Sydney: the accidental city since 1788*, Hale & Iremonger, Sydney, 1993, 128 pp

Broomham, Rosemary, *Vital Connections: a history of New South Wales roads from 1788*, Hale & Iremonger, Sydney, 2001, 212 pp

de Marco, Chris and Spearritt, Peter, *Planning Sydney's Future*, Allen & Unwin, Sydney, 1988, 160 pp

Gibbons, Robert, 'The Fall of the Giant: trams versus trains and buses in Sydney 1900–1961' in Garry Wotherspoon (ed), *Sydney's Transport*, Hale & Iremonger, Sydney, 1983

Gunn, John, *Along Parallel Lines: a history of the railways of New South Wales 1850–1986*, MUP, Melbourne, 1989, 581 pp

Keenan, David, *Tramways of Sydney*, Transit, 1979, 88 pp

Poulsen, Michael and Spearritt, Peter, *Sydney: a social and political atlas*, Allen & Unwin, Sydney, 1981, 164 pp

Art, photography and film

Duggan, Laurie, *Ghost Nation: imagined space and Australian visual culture 1901–1939*, UQP, Brisbane, 2001, 292 pp

Dupain, Max and Tanner, Howard, *Building the Sydney Harbour Bridge: the photography of Henri Mallard*, Sun Books, Melbourne, 1976

Jacobsen, Lennart, 'The Polysemous Coathanger: the Sydney Harbour Bridge in feature film, 1930–1982' <http://www.sensesofcinema.com>

McGrath, Sandra and Walker, Robert, *Sydney Harbour Paintings from 1794*, Jacaranda, Brisbane, 1979, 112 pp

Prunster, Ursula, *The Sydney Harbour Bridge 1932–1982*, Angus & Robertson, Sydney, 1982, 134 pp

Spencer, Gwen Morton and Ure Smith, Sam (eds), *Portrait of Sydney*, Ure Smith, Sydney, 1952, 48 pp (opening essay by Kenneth Slessor, book includes photographs by Max Dupain, David Moore and Rob Hillier)

'The Sydney Harbour Bridge', *Henri Mallard Catalogue*, Australian Centre

for Photography, Sydney, 2002

Willis, Anne-Marie, *Picturing Australia: a history of photography*, Angus & Robertson, Sydney, 1988, 304 pp

Wilson, Gavin, *Harbourlights: the life and times of Peter Kingston*, Craftsman House, Melbourne, 2004, 183 pp

Bridges

Most of the world's great bridges now have at least one authoritative website outlining their construction and history.

McCullough, David, *The Great Bridge*, Simon and Schuster, New York, 1972 (on the Brooklyn Bridge)

Rastorfer, Darl, *Six Bridges: the legacy of Othmar H Ammann*, Yale University Press, New Haven, 2000, 188 pp (chapters on each of Ammann's six bridges, including the Bayonne Bridge)

Tourism, Sydney–Melbourne rivalry and the Sydney Opera House

Davidson, Jim (ed), *The Sydney–Melbourne Book*, Allen & Unwin, Sydney, 1986, 337 pp (including the chapter on 'City Images')

Harper, Melissa and White, Richard (eds), *Symbols of Australia*, UNSW Press, Sydney, 2010, 240 pp

Messent, David, *Opera House Act One*, Messent, Sydney, 1997, 544 pp (there is a huge amount of literature on the Sydney Opera House. This book includes a bibliography of earlier histories and assessments)

Spearritt, Peter, 'Celebration of a Nation: the triumph of spectacle' in S Janson and S Macintyre (eds), *Making the Bicentenary*, Australian Historical Studies, Melbourne, 1988, pp 3–20

Novels

Hundreds of novels are set in Sydney and many of these feature the Bridge. A handful of the more notable over the last 80 years include:

Corris, Peter, *Wet Graves*, Bantam,

Sydney, 1991, 242 pp (a novel
featuring detective Cliff Hardy
which delves into the lives of Bridge
builders and their offspring)
Dark, Eleanor, *Waterway*, Macmillan,
New York, 1938, 445 pp
Elliott, Sumner Locke, *Water Under the
Bridge*, Hamilton, London, 1978, 367
pp
Mackenzie, Seaforth, *The Refuge*, Angus
& Robertson, Sydney, 1954, 343 pp

The Sydney Harbour Tunnel

Feizkhah, Elizabeth, *The Story of the
Sydney Harbour Tunnel*, Ironbark Press,
Randwick, 1992, 128 pp
'Proposed Sydney Harbour Tunnel:
environmental impact assessment',
Department of Environment and
Planning, Sydney, 1987, 103 pp
*Sydney Harbour Tunnel Official Souvenir
Publication*, Taylor Marketing, Sydney,
1992, 64 pp
Thomas, Maree and Spearritt, Peter,
'Celebrating One Bridge, Fighting
Another', *The Sydney Gazette*, no
5, December 1982, pp 2–6 (a
publication of the Sydney History
Group)

Heritage and conservation

Heritage Group, Department of
Public Works, *Sydney Harbour Bridge
Conservation Management Plan*, Roads and
Traffic Authority, Sydney, 1998, 178
pp. (Revised version, by Godden
Mackay Logan, RTA 2007, 247 pp).
Meredith Walker nominated the
Bridge for the New South Wales
National Trust Register in 1974.

A note on websites

All websites appearing in 'Sources
and further reading' were correct as
at July 2011. Readers are advised that
website addresses change from time
to time.

Copyright, artwork

I am grateful to copyright holders who
have given permission for the repro-
duction of paintings, photo-graphs,
posters , cartoons, graphic images and
caricatures. Every effort has been
made to identify and contact copyright
holders. I thank the Cazneaux family,
Lisa Moore (John D Moore and David

The Spectre, the Bridge from York Street by Cazneaux. *The Bridge Book,* Art in
Australia, 1930, courtesy Cazneaux family

Moore),Judith Murray (Roland
Wakelin), the late Neil Curtis, Ann
Mills (Grace Cossington Smith), Robin
Moore (Emerson Curtis), Viscopy
(W.E. Pidgeon, Margaret Preston).

I would also like to thank State
Records New South Wales, the
Historic Houses Trust (Museum of
Sydney), the National Gallery of
Victoria, the Art Gallery of NSW, the
Art Gallery of South Australia, the
Sydney Morning Herald and News
Limited.

Catalogue entries for the major
paintings reproduced are listed here:

Grace Cossington SMITH
Australia 1892-1984
The bridge in-curve (1930)
Tempera on cardboard
83.6 x 111.8 cm
Presented by the National Gallery

Society of Victoria, 1967
National Gallery of Victoria, Melbourne

Roland WAKELIN
born New Zealand 1887, arrived
Australia 1912, died 1971
The bridge under construction (1928-29)
oil on canvas board
100.0 x 120.0 cm
Purchased, 1967
National Gallery of Victoria,
Melbourne

Margaret PRESTON
Sydney Bridge, (c 1932)
Woodcut, black ink, hand coloured
with gouche on cream Japanese laid
paper, 19.0 x 23.2cm blockmark; 22.7
x 31.9cm sheet (irreg.)
Purchased 1964
Collection: Art Gallery of New South
Wales
© Margaret Preston Estate
Photograph: Jenni Carter
[accn # DA30.1964]

John D. MOORE
Sydney Harbour, 1936
oil on canvas, 91.5 x 122.5m stretcher,
119.5 x 6.5cm frame
Purchased 1936
Collection: Art Gallery of New South
Wales
© David Moore
Photograph: Paula Bray
[accn # 6382]

Dorrit BLACK
Australia, 1891-1951
The Bridge, 1930, Sydney
oil on canvas on board
60.0 x 81.0 cm
Bequest of the artist 1951
Art Gallery of South Australia,
Adelaide

Sydney Ure SMITH
Australia, 1887–1949
*Sydney Harbour Bridge from West Circular
Quay*
watercolour and pencil
42.2 x 32.0 cm
National Gallery of Victoria,
Melbourne
Felton Bequest, 1931

Roland WAKELIN
The Bridge from North Sydney
1939
Courtesy of Judith Murray, Leslie
Walton

171

A Souvenir
of Beautiful
SYDNEY

14 Specially Selected Views in Full Color

The pylons were not regularly steam-cleaned until the 1960s. Concertina postcard folder c 1955. Spearritt collection

In choosing an image for their annual fashion festival catalogue, 1937, the department store Farmer's chose to have Father Christmas suspended above a twinkling Sydney. Spearritt collection

175